PURE

The Life Changing Power of Uncontaminated Grace

GRACE

Clark Whitten

DESTINY IMAGE® PUBLISHERS, INC.
P.O. Box 310, Shippensburg, PA 17257-0310

"Promoting Inspired Lives."

This book and all other Destiny Image, Revival Press, MercyPlace, Fresh Bread, Destiny Image Fiction, and Treasure House books are available at Christian bookstores and distributors worldwide.

For a U.S. bookstore nearest you, call 1-800-722-6774.
For more information on foreign distributors, call 717-532-3040.
Reach us on the Internet: www.destinyimage.com.

ISBN 13 TP: 978-0-7684-4104-8
ISBN 13 Ebook: 978-0-7684-8862-3

For Worldwide Distribution, Printed in the U.S.A.
6 7 / 15 14

Dedication

To Martha, my beloved wife and partner on the journey of discovering this great truth. Your life looks a lot like His to me.

To Grace Church, my family of faith, without whom this book might never have been. Your hunger for truth inspires me, and your unabashed support humbles me.

Acknowledgments

My first acknowledgment is to my friend, James Barron. Thank you, my dear brother, for all you have taught me about the finished work of Christ and for your relentless resistance to legalism in all its forms. You are a hero to all of us at Grace Church and to many more in the Body of Christ at large.

To my spiritual father, Jack Taylor. Thank you for your encouragement to write what you saw as an important addition to what has already been said. I love you, Pop!

To Don Milam at Destiny Image, thanks for taking a chance on a first-time author and for encouraging me to finish what I had begun.

To Mark and Amadita Stone, thank you seems inadequate for your generosity and unfailing support. Your help was more important than you know.

To all my ministry "buds" out there who challenged and encouraged me—David Smith, Robert Morris, Tom Lane, David Loveless, Wayne Drain, Jimmy Evans, Ed Ivie, Brady Boyd, Alan Chambers, Bo Williams, Dudley Hall, and James Robison.

Last but certainly not least, to my dear family who inspired me daily to put into print what they heard me say. Thank you, dear ones, for believing in me. Without you, there would be no Grace Church and probably no book! I love you beyond words—Martha, Wendy and Joey, Abby and Heath, John and Valli, Clark, Luke, John, and Shelby.

Endorsements

Pastor Clark Whitten writes from a depth of experience, strong scholarship and prophetic revelation about Grace. This book is simply profound. Clark looks at the profound implications of God's grace in a simple, down to earth way. These pages are both challenging and understandable. I don't know anyone who would say they truly understand the vastness of God's grace. Clark gets as close as I've seen.

E. Wayne Drain
Senior Pastor, Fellowship of Christians

Nothing has transformed every part of who I am and what I do like grace. One man has helped me understand it in a way that has made a profound difference altering the course of my life, my walk with Christ and my ministry: Clark Whitten. Everything he has taught me over the last 16 years is now in this incredible book, *Pure Grace*. I'm begging you to read it, apply it and live it. It will make all the difference in the world. To say that I recommend it is the understatement of the century.

Alan Chambers
President, Exodus International

Years ago I heard Clark Whitten preach on grace and I knew that he was a man in the grip of one great truth. His call to "pure" grace is a refreshing and much-needed immersion in a healing stream. Grace unalloyed by all that legalists might wish to add to it, grace as pure as the very nature of God, that's the grace I need and that's Whitten's message.

Dr. Mark Rutland
President, Oral Roberts University

The first time I heard Clark teach on grace, everything within me thought, "This is too good to be true!" But it is true! And receiving the truth about grace has produced more love, joy, peace, righteousness, and faith in my life than anything else. The greatest burden I carry as a pastor and an author is to help people understand how good grace really is. Clark Whitten is the best teacher I have ever heard on the subject of 'Pure Grace.' This is truly a book that will change your life, guaranteed!

Robert Morris
Senior Pastor, Gateway Church - Southlake, Texas
Author of *The Blessed Life*

Clark Whitten understands grace—a foreign concept among many believers today. Grace is not works, but it certainly works the very life and transforming power of God into our lives. The church needs to recognize the need to walk in this power. Once we grasp the true meaning of grace, we'll live not as orphans, but as children of God.

James Robison
Founder, LIFE Outreach International
Fort Worth, Texas

If you're like me, there are few things I can remember that people said more than 20 years ago, unless it was life defining. But more than 20 years ago, while listening to Clark Whitten teach on grace he said these words: "Most people know how to be 'good DOERS' but few people have learned to be 'good RECEIVERS.'" Those words punctured my performance driven heart, and became a divine magnet that God has used to 'draw' me to Himself in life-changing ways. When I heard that Clark was putting in writing the biblical grace concepts that I've heard him share, and watched him live, I was extremely excited for you, the reader. If you need a fresh drink of living water from a very deep well that will last beyond a lifetime, then read this book. As you learn to DO LESS and RECEIVE MORE, few things will revolutionize you more.

David Loveless
Lead Pastor, Discovery Church
Orlando, Florida

Clark Whitten has taught me more about grace than any other person. I was sitting in a crowd listening to him at a men's retreat in Colorado when God wrecked my heart. I hope this book does the same for you.

Brady Boyd
Pastor, New Life Church
Author of *Fear No Evil*

One of the greatest gifts God has ever given to me is my friendship with Clark Whitten. Without a doubt, he is the greatest authority on the subject of grace I know. Over the past 28 years of our friendship I have heard Clark preach many sermons on grace. It has set me free and allowed me to understand and experience God in new and greater ways. *Pure Grace* is one of the best books I have ever read. I couldn't put it down! Reading this book will change your life. You will never be the same.

Jimmy Evans
Founder and CEO, Marriage Today
Senior Pastor, Trinity Fellowship Church

I am thrilled with the publishing of Clark Whitten's *Pure Grace*. This has been the core of Clark's message for a long time. It is not some novel interpretation he has recently discovered. He has lived it, as well as proclaimed it, for many years. I agree with him that the contemporary gospel being promoted is a pale mixture of law and grace. It does not honor the God of grace nor transform those who embrace it. It produces a religious facade that makes followers sad and detractors mad. I pray that many will read *Pure Grace* and experience the heart of the gospel that changes people and glorifies God.

Dudley Hall
President of Successful Christian Living Ministries
Author of *Grace Works*

Contents

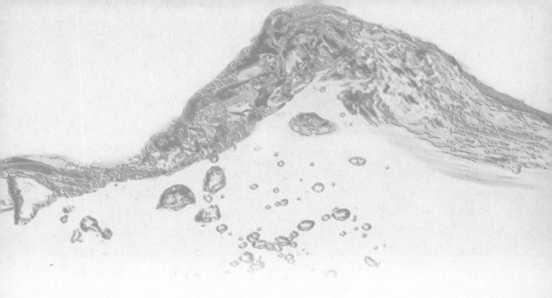

Foreword

"Simply profound and profoundly simple" are terms that describe the volume you hold in you hands. You are about to embark on a journey of fantastic and believable truths that will affect every part of your life for the remainder of your life.

Clark Whitten dares to "tell it like it is" with confidence and clarity. He will draw criticism from those who thought that goodness on their part helped God decide to "save" them or think they must perform correctly to retain the gift of salvation.

The title *Pure Grace* does not suggest that there are gradations of grace, but it does suggest the need of caution to guard against something that is impure masquerading as grace. This book says it loudly in many different ways, "That which makes salvation less than salvation is not grace, it is ungrace or disgrace." That which does not convey God as infinitely gracious, eternally gracious, and stubbornly gracious is not grace at all.

Yes, many a soul will respond to this work on grace with, "Wait a minute, does that mean that God winks at sin, dilutes His moral expectations of humankind and forgets justice altogether?" (By the way this is an acceptable question, not because the answer is yes but because the right answer clarifies the grace question.) Grace flat out declares that God in Christ has forever settled every issue that stands between a sinner and Himself! Forever! Completely! A new creation has emerged in whom old things are passed away—are no more to such a degree that they have never been; remembered no more by our omniscient God.

Grace with conditions that depend on humanity's performance to stay in it is no grace at all. Grace, so called, that is uncertain, conditional, or fearful is flat out *no grace at all. Period! Exclamation mark!*

So pure grace is true grace, God's grace—all other forms that appear to be grace are pretenders, faux appearances. The Kingdom of God, His gracious and absolute rule of everything and everybody for all time and eternity, is a Kingdom of grace.

Yes, as Clark suggests early, the words "too good to be true" will be heard of this powerful concept. It is virtually inevitable. I have read it, some parts of it several times. I've been moved to think, *Maybe this is a bit strong and stark here.* But when the day is done and the evidence is in, real grace, pure grace wins! I agree with it, every word of it and am happily and heartily blessed by it. Of all the acrostics attempting to define grace, a new one has emerged:

God's
Real
Attitude
Clearly
Expressed

After all it was He who said to Paul in deep crisis, "My grace is sufficient."

Jack Taylor
Dimensions Ministries
Melbourne, Florida

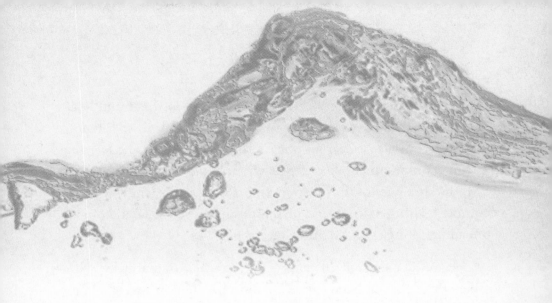

Introduction

"Grace is too good to be true! And if it *is* true, why haven't we heard about it before now? Why hasn't what you teach been taught to us by our pastors and theologians? What you teach intrigues me, but it cannot be that good or that easy! Doesn't God care about how we act?"

These are fairly typical responses from a believer who has attended an Evangelical Christian church for many years when confronted with the truth about the finished work of Christ. It *does* seem too good to be true. But it *is* true! Liberty, freedom, joy, spiritual passion, hope, and a host of other benefits are produced by a revelation of grace. If spiritual revival—renewal of spiritual life—is something to be desired, then an understanding of grace is the answer.

Some statements and concepts you will read in this humble attempt to explain the near unexplainable may shock your religious sensibilities, but please hear me out. I have been teaching and learning this stuff for more than two decades, and it has dramatically changed my life and the lives of those around me. Grace is the gateway to our becoming fruitful, mature, and joyous disciples. Being a child of God is fun and exciting again! Remember?

I became a believer at 20 years of age—rather dramatically, without benefit of having been raised in church. I felt an incredible joy and sense of belonging, acceptance, and love from my new heavenly Father. My relationship with Him was simple and emotionally overwhelming. Witnessing to my friends and family about Christ was natural, exciting, and very effective. I loved God and He loved me. There was no sense at all of having to justify His love by doing anything. Kind of like Adam and Eve before the Fall, huh? They just were who they were created to be. They were human beings in intimate relationship with this incredible God. That is how I felt.

Until…I began attending church and being taught by people who were in bondage to a lie. They didn't know it and neither did I. It wasn't their fault, and I don't hold any grudges; they were doing the best they could with the revelation they had, and their motives were pure.

However, the impact of their legalism and performance model of Christianity was devastating. My fresh new joy and enthusiasm began to be replaced by guilt and a focus on being a "good boy" for God. I noticed a growing sense of alienation from my heavenly Father and my prayer life changed from adoration and wonder to a series of sterile "I'm sorries" for being a bad boy.

Along the way throughout the years came a number of achievements that others admired and about which I was proud—but there was a lingering sense I did them mostly on my own. Honestly, my family, my church, and my friends all paid a price for the lie I had believed. The Clark who Jesus died to redeem, the Clark I was created to be, was locked up in a prison of lies. My personality, my gifting, and my destiny were all a shadow of that newly emerging, life-filled, joyous spiritual babe who intuitively got it right for a while.

Today I feel like I have come full circle! I love God and He loves me! As Paul said, I have recaptured the simplicity of my devotion to Christ. You will too, when you see it. I'm certain. You were made for this stuff! It makes sense for the one who gets it. It has the power to infuse you with hope that you can become like Jesus here on earth. While that is not a goal to be achieved, it is certainly a promise to be received. When you see it, you will see it. I hope you will look so you can see.

Conscious and Unconscious

OK. Allow me to make a few statements that should pique your curiosity, then we will get to the teaching.

1. Christians are way too conscious of sin and way too unconscious of God's grace. Listen, Jesus did not die to modify your behavior! He could have achieved behavior modification in any number of ways that wouldn't have cost Him His life. Jesus went to the cross taking the sins of the world upon Himself. All of yours and mine were included! All of them—past, present, and future. We stand before God's throne of grace sinless. That has to be true, or we don't stand there at all. Interested in exploring that? We will.

2. Christians are not required to confess their sins to God in order to be forgiven, we already are forgiven. With the exception of First John 1:9, there is no biblical basis for a believer to confess sins to God for forgiveness. To each other for healing, yes; but not to God for forgiveness. How much time will that free up!

3. Legalistic Christianity is in the sin management business full-time and failing miserably at the job. While sin management may be lucrative, it is entirely ineffective. Sin cannot be managed. Still, the Church continues to employ this model of ministry.

4. I believe that New Testament repentance is not the Holy Spirit convicting of sin, me feeling sorry, confessing the sin, asking for forgiveness, and committing to stop doing it. That typical scenario is a grotesque misrepresentation of the gift of repentance. It is heathenish! What is God really asking of me if He asks me to repent? We will see.

5. Contrary to popular religious opinion, God is not angry toward me and never will be. Not in the least. He was angry, but no longer. All of His anger—sense of violation because of sin—was poured out and extinguished on His dear Son. He is not going to "get me" because I have sinned. He "got" Jesus for my sin! My bad works don't move God any more than my good works move Him. He simply isn't moved by "works" of any kind. If you are motivated to do a great work for God, good luck!

6. "Do good, God is glad; do bad, God is mad" is the M.O. of legalistic Christianity. I curry favor with God by good works and incur His displeasure by sinning. Honestly, what does that sound like? Islam? Buddhism?

African fetish worship? It is utterly heathenish and deadly wrong. If you can't take it that far, at least agree it is foolish. Galatians 3:1-3 makes that clear:

You foolish Galatians, who has bewitched you, before whose eyes Jesus Christ was publicly portrayed as crucified? This is the only thing I want to find out from you: did you receive the Spirit by the works of the Law, or by hearing with faith? Are you so foolish? Having begun by the Spirit, are you now being perfected by the flesh?

7. Sin, for the Christian, is a violation of friendship—relationship—not a violation of the law. Christians are not under the jurisdiction of the Old Testament law. Many believe and teach grace without law is a pathway to sinful behavior. They see grace and law as "balance." The Apostle Paul saw it as "mixture." I have heard some refer to New Testament grace as "greasy grace." That term offends me at a level I cannot describe! The truth is, anyone who clings to this "mixture theory of grace and law" doesn't trust the power of love to transform lives. They don't see that the power of relationship and intimacy with God can be trusted to transform a human being. God can be trusted! Paul said that a little leaven leavens the whole lump. He was referring to a little law leavening the whole lump of grace. What most of us have been taught about what God is like and what He desires from us simply is not true. It is much harder to sin against love than law.

8. Many think and teach that while sin doesn't destroy my relationship with God as a believer, it does damage my fellowship with God implying God punishes or disciplines

me for sin by withdrawing His fellowship. Some mental gymnastics are required to arrive at this conclusion, but keeping people under the thumb of God is necessary to make them behave and, after all, behavior control is the goal. The threat of God withholding fellowship while remaining in relationship is another non-biblical concept. It is a lie. Show me where the New Testament even hints at such a thing. The opposite is true.

Listen, *everything changed in the New Covenant!* We are seated together with Christ in heavenly places now—no withdrawing of fellowship as a means of punishment. I am convinced, Paul says, nothing can separate me from the love of God (see Rom. 8:39). You may have thought what you did separated you from God's love, but it did not. *Nothing* can separate us from His love.

9. Christians are truly free. We are free to laugh or cry, read a novel or the Bible, eat meat offered to idols or avoid it, drink wine or water, smoke or chew, get fat or fit, attend church or stay at home, tithe or give nothing—all without condemnation from God. There is no condemnation for those who are in Christ (see Rom. 8:1) doesn't mean no consequences or loss, but does mean no condemnation.

God has the power to change my "wanter." As that happens, I get to do what I want! My brother spent several years in jail, and he said the worst part of that experience was never getting to do what he wanted. Doesn't that sound like our spiritual jails? Look, I'm not minimizing the impact of sin, but I am confident in the power of love to change us from the inside out. Paul said we were not to use our liberty as an occasion for the flesh, but we all do at times. Our liberty isn't negated by our sin any more than it was procured by our good behavior. Only free people can become more free! Legalists have no chance of standing in liberty. They have none to begin with.

Before we move on to the teaching, I have an idea I want to float by you. I believe the Body of Christ is on the threshold of a new reformation that will impact the world beyond what the Protestant Reformation accomplished. Luther and Calvin got it right concerning justification by faith, and that resurrected truth revolutionized the Church and the world. However, they didn't get it right concerning sanctification. Their approach sounds familiar: One is saved by grace through faith (justified) but made perfect (sanctified) by human effort through law-keeping.

Saved by grace, perfected by the flesh. Little has changed in 500 years! The Church still employs that same strategy and deeply believes it is biblical truth. The rules may have changed some, but the approach is the same. When the Church gets the revelation that we are sanctified—actually it has already happened—by the same process as justification, grace through faith, a reformation that will again change the world is at hand. It is already beginning here and there and will become a tsunami of joy and spiritual passion as more and more believers begin to free themselves of legalism. The religious establishment will, by and large, resist with gnashing of teeth, but the inevitable move of God characterized by grace is on the way.

Get ready! This reformation will reveal the Father and His great love for His children. Evangelism will change, fellowship between us will deepen and be much more meaningful, and aggressive love will sweep millions into the Kingdom. The Gospel will once again become truly Good News! There is a party being hosted by our heavenly Father in honor of those of us who have come to our senses in the pig pen of legalism and decided to come home to be with Him.

There is an engraved invitation with your name on it. I sincerely pray you might lay down whatever defenses you have and open your heart to the revelation of *pure grace*.

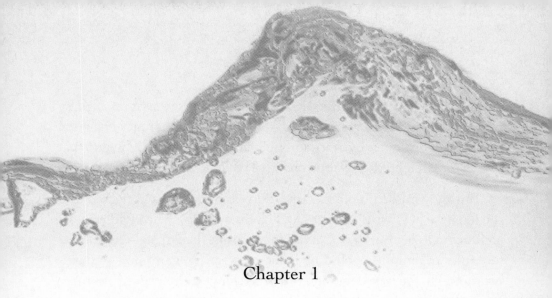

Chapter 1

A Grace Reformation

A little leaven leavens the whole lump of dough.
—*Galatians 5:9*

Little has changed in the Protestant church in more than 500 years. Some of the rules have been modified and adapted to present culture, some methods and strategies of conducting church have changed slightly; but in reality, our core approach to reaching and discipling people is the same as it was 500 years ago.

Martin Luther and John Calvin, the primary leaders of the Protestant Reformation, got it right concerning justification, or how one is saved. *"The righteous man shall live by faith"* (Gal. 3:11) was the revelation Luther discovered and he and Calvin preached. In their break with Catholicism, they correctly saw that no one is saved or justified by rule-keeping, church attendance, or adherence to external behavioral demands. Salvation is by grace through faith. They got it right, and that Holy Spirit-inspired revelation changed the world.

But they missed it on sanctification, or how one is perfected into the likeness of Christ. Luther and Calvin both drew up rigid rules of conduct in their churches. Calvin, for example, had a catalogue of austere rules of morality including bans on swearing, gambling, and fornication. He forbade dancing even at weddings. Unexcused absences from worship services were severely penalized. Adultery and homosexuality could draw severe sentences, even death. (Notice there were no rules against alcohol consumption. I wonder if it had to do with the fact that Luther had a little drinking problem? Just a thought.)

It has been long rumored that Luther's view of Christians was that we are piles of dung covered with snow! If he actually said this, I think he had a very low view of the miracle of the new birth and would agree with modern religious thinking that Christians are simply sinners saved by grace—an unbiblical but widely held view of salvation. This is the kind of legalistic leaven that has leavened the modern Church's doctrine and caused Christians to have a low view of salvation themselves with tragic results.

If you are a sinner, you have not been saved by grace! If you have been saved by grace, you are not a sinner! We will cover this topic more thoroughly in a later chapter as we consider the implications of righteousness, but allow me to be a bit repetitive because of the importance of this subject. If you have been "saved by grace," you were a sinner—but now you are something else entirely!

Paul addresses Christians as saints in many of his letters, and never uses the term "sinner" to identify believers. We are talking about a state of being, not an act or an action when we use the term "sinner." We were born with a sin nature, and that is precisely why we had to be born again. My new nature is not a sin nature but a sinless nature! I can sin, but I am not a sinner. All of us are either in Adam (with a sin nature) or in Christ (with a sinless nature). There are no other categories! *A state of being!* Saints or sinners. Saints can sin, but that sin does not undo the work of Christ and make a saint a sinner. A sinner can do good works, but good works do not make a sinner a saint. See?

Here is the approach Luther and Calvin took. One is saved by grace through faith, but then for the rest of our earthly lives we must try our best to modify our behavior to please God and release His blessing in our lives. To be pleasing to God or "right" with God depends on my behavior—do my best to keep the rules here and hang on until I get to Heaven—then I will be fully sanctified.

Oh, by the way, many of the rules are not even closely related to Scripture, which is the M.O. of legalism. As I said in the beginning of the chapter, little has changed in the Protestant church in 500 years! Walk into almost any Protestant church and you will soon hear a mixture of law and grace taught and received with great enthusiasm, agreement, and amens all around! It doesn't matter what flavor of church: Evangelical, Charismatic, Pentecostal, denominational, nondenominational, Reformed or Free Will, seeker-sensitive, fundamental, or liberal. At the end of the day, almost all are presenting a version of the Gospel leavened with the law.

The leaven of the law is found in even the most gracious presentation of the Gospel:

- Get saved by grace through faith, then act right and try hard to be like Jesus because the world is watching, and you must not let them see you sin. Help out God in His mission to rid the earth of sin. Oh, by the way, we will help you with your list of rules so you won't be confused about what is required of you. Do these things and you might even get blessed by this capricious God we serve.

- You must die daily to accomplish all God wants of you and serve Him fervently and thus prove to be a good disciple. Stop sinning and be good. After all Jesus has done for you, it is a small thing to ask. When you are bad, come to the altar and get right with God. He will forgive you again and might even bless you if you will get serious about changing. Set your will to do what is right and thus glorify God. Confess your sin to God daily and pray for forgiveness so you can start the day clean. Stay up-to-date in your confession and repentance; and whatever you do, don't have too much fun!

- The Bible is a perfect rule book, so read it daily for instruction on how to act. The Holy Spirit was given to you to empower you to act better and better and convict you of your sin when you stray. God is pleased when you act right. When you don't, He will clean your clock! Fear God and keep His commandments. Amen.

- Oh, I almost forgot, tell somebody this week about how to be saved and happy like we are!

Religion—not real Christianity—is and always has been in the behavior modification and sin management business. It is so lucrative and so firmly entrenched in the Church that it will take a second Great Reformation and a revelation of no less importance than Luther's to correct this great and spiritually murderous lie. What this "saved by grace but perfected by human effort" approach has done is produce a Church that is judgmental, angry, hopeless, helpless, dependent, fearful, uninspired, ineffective, and perpetually spiritually immature. The only bright spot is the hope of Heaven, and even that isn't certain to the average Evangelical Christian. No wonder we haven't impacted our culture and have become a joke to most casual observers.

But that is not the most heartbreaking result of this religious lie. The most heartbreaking result is the personal devastation that comes when sincere, pure-hearted people attempt the impossible over and over again and are beaten and bloodied by their efforts to please God. I don't blame them for giving up, checking out, or playing the game. Failure gets old fast. Instead of correctly representing and displaying the great good news of the Gospel and the joy of our magnificent Savior, our lives, regardless of how sincere we are, simply do not correctly reflect Him when we are trapped in the lie of legalism. I hate what religious legalism is and has done to deflect His glory and enslave those Jesus died to set free. Religion has always been the greatest enemy of the true Gospel and the finished work of Christ.

Listen, *Jesus did not die to modify my behavior!* If behavior modification had been His ultimate purpose, He could have accomplished it in any number of ways short of sacrificing His life. Changing my behavior is a small thing to the Creator of the universe. *Jesus died to take the sins of the world upon Himself and redeem everyone who will believe.* Jesus died to transform people into children of God, to create something new and holy that can be in union with a Holy God. I am not waiting or working to be justified. I am already justified, and get this—I am already sanctified! Sanctification—having been made perfect—is a state of being, not a goal to be achieved or grow into. *"For by one offering He has perfected for all time those who are sanctified"* (Heb. 10:14).

The old religious approach of "I *am* justified, I *am being* sanctified, and I *will be* glorified" is a lie. It is religious nonsense. Progressive sanctification is based on the theory that we can act better and better until we get to be almost like Jesus on earth, then be fully made perfect in Heaven. Listen, I believe that if you aren't made perfect now, you cannot be in union with God, and you won't go to Heaven! No unsanctified person or thing can live in God's presence. God will not do anything to me in Heaven that He hasn't already done here!

Let's look at what really happened to me when I was born again and what Jesus had to accomplish to bring me into union with my heavenly Father. It is not what most think, and it certainly is not what religion teaches. It is bigger, better, more far-reaching, and more permanent than most anyone believes. Grace is better than we think. The finished work of Christ is more complete than we have dared to dream.

A RADICAL PLAN

What is salvation? Many would say it is getting me out of earth and into Heaven, but that is not salvation. It may be one result of salvation, but it is not salvation. Salvation is not getting me out of earth and into Heaven; *salvation is getting God out of Heaven and into me!* God had to prepare me for His presence. When I was saved, I became the temple of the Holy Spirit. I came into union with Christ, and I became a son of God. Now, friends, that took some doing on God's part! For Him to make me into something He could dwell in took a sacrifice beyond my comprehension but He did it! *It is finished!* "*Christ in you, the hope of glory,*" Paul says in Colossians 1:27.

What God had to do was radical. It was cataclysmic. He had to create something new. He had to create a new person who was a perfect dwelling place for His Spirit; and that is exactly what He did. He did not redo the old or remodel or tweak me here and there. I had to become a "new creation!" I had to be "born again." I was dead in my sin and had to be raised to new life. My sin could not accompany me into God's presence, and because God's goal was union with me, He could not simply cover my sin as in the Old Covenant. He had to cleanse me of my sin. *"Though your sins are as scarlet, they will be as white as snow"* (Isa. 1:18).

I could not be conformed, I had to be transformed. "Conform" comes from the Greek word *morph* or *morpha*. It means to "shape into" or take the substance that is and shape it or mold it into some other form, but the substance remains the same. "Transform" comes from the Greek words *meta morph* from which we get the English "metamorphosis." It means to be "changed over."[1] Not only is the form new, the substance is new also. Metamorphosis produces a new substance, a new thing, or a new being.

The old me could not be conformed to the likeness of Christ. All things must become new. That is precisely what Jesus accomplished in me, and in you if you are born again! All things new. I was dead in my sin but now I am alive in Christ. I was a slave, had no relationship with God, now I am a son—and if a son, an heir of God. I was a citizen of the kingdom of darkness, now I am a citizen of the Kingdom of God. I was born of the flesh but reborn of the Spirit. I was a stranger and an alien to God, now I draw close to Him and am already seated at His right hand with Christ. Radical change! Transformed! *"Therefore if anyone is in Christ, he is a new creature; the old things passed away; behold, new things have come"* (2 Cor. 5:17).

What I am talking about is a state of being, not a goal to be achieved. I *am* all these things, I'm not waiting to become them. It has to be this way. Our Holy God cannot, will not, allow sin in His presence. To be in His presence, I must be as sinless as Christ. Again, that is a state of being that Christ accomplished in me. That is why I believe progressive sanctification is nonsense. It is a religious teaching to control behavior and manage sin. Legalists and religionists simply do not trust in the finished work of Christ and the efficacy of His blood to produce His intended result. Therefore, they feel compelled to help Him control the behavior of His new creations.

The apostle Paul came against the same insidious lie and addressed the problem in Galatians 3:1-3:

> *You foolish Galatians, who has bewitched you, before whose eyes Jesus Christ was publicly portrayed as crucified? This is the only thing I want to find out from you; did you receive the Spirit by works of the Law, or by hearing with faith? Are you so foolish? Having begun by the Spirit, are you now being perfected by the flesh?*

Paul calls the Galatian Christians foolish! It is foolishness to believe one is perfected in a manner other than the manner in which one is saved or justified. They were saved; they received the Spirit, by hearing with faith—and they are perfected, sanctified, the same way! He asks who bewitched them. Who lied to you about this? Who tricked you into believing this foolishness? The flesh cannot—ever—produce the level of perfection God requires to be in union with Him.

Legalism and its twin brother religion always appeal to the flesh. May I say both are deadly and always at cross purposes to life, liberty, and the pursuit of freedom, joy, godliness, holiness, Christ-likeness, spiritual maturity, and intimacy with God. If you have a desire to experience the abundant life Jesus died to give you and to truly reflect His glory to those around you, you must refuse and resist these two deadly enemies of truth and open your eyes to see the magnificent and completed work of Christ on your behalf. We must see and believe who Christ has made us to be in order to live out this glorious life He not only modeled for us but empowers us to live.

Because He Is, I Am

I am justified! I am a son of God! I am an heir of God and a joint heir with Christ! I am cleansed of my sin! I am a new creature! I am righteous! I am holy and blameless! I am part of a royal priesthood and a holy nation! I am a living stone in His temple! I am His beloved Body and Bride! I am the repository of His Spirit! I am *sanctified!*

I am not hoping these things will happen, waiting for them to happen, working on them, praying for them, or seeking them. I am not attempting to achieve them even with God's help. I have stopped listening to those who deny my sanctification, and I am proudly proclaiming it. I admit to being deeply humbled by it and don't fully understand it; but I believe it, and it has changed my life. I am sanctified. I cannot add anything to the finished work of Christ and any attempt on my part to do so is foolishness of the highest degree and always ends in defeat. He did it.

I am sanctified.

If that is not true, everything in the Bible could be a lie. It simply has to be this way. Don't misunderstand me. I am not saying my flesh is sanctified. It is not. There is no good thing in my flesh. Please do not connect the two. Clark's flesh and Clark are not the same. My flesh has no power to accomplish any godly thing, and that is precisely why human performance and law-keeping always fail in attempts to be good enough. It cannot be good because it is not good. Our hope of becoming like Jesus is in our understanding that we already are like Him. We are sanctified.

I believe this truth has been a stumbling block to the Church and to individual Christians for centuries and has kept us mired in the mud of legalism and human effort. The finished work of Christ on our behalf is so good and so complete, we cannot allow ourselves to believe it! If the devil couldn't keep us from the revelation of being saved by grace through faith, and he obviously couldn't thanks to Luther, Calvin, and others, his fallback strategy was to limit the damage done by deceiving us about the completeness of Christ's work. His strategy was brilliant in its simplicity. He lied to us again about God—remember Eve. God loved us enough to save us, but now we are under obligation to be good so we can have His favor. Saved by grace, but perfected through the flesh has been the devil's strategy from the beginning!

Recently a man in our church said to me something like this, "You know, Pastor, I think we have been praying for the wrong thing for years. We have prayed for spiritual revival and what we had in mind is not what God wants. Revival to us is rededicated flesh and a renewed commitment to doing good things for God. You know, acting better and doing more. I don't think that is real revival."

I believe Bill was right. I asked him if what he was presently experiencing felt like revival, renewal of life, and he said, "Absolutely"!

"What brought it about?" I asked.

He replied, "A growing understanding of grace and the completed work of Christ. I am seeing truth, and it is changing my life."

Grace produces perpetual spiritual life and vitality and moves us toward spiritual maturity. Legalism and religion produce perpetual spiritual immaturity—the immature look for authority figures to tell them what to do. Immature authority figures make rules that benefit themselves or their institutions and secure their power and control. It is like leaving a 5-year-old in charge of a 2-year-old!

While I may be exaggerating a bit, this scenario sounds like today's Church to me, and I have extensive experience in church! Just like immature children, we want to know the rules primarily to see what we can get away with. What can I get away with and still be in God's good graces. There is little awe and wonder at the magnificence of God, and we are reduced to trying as best we can to get by until we get to Heaven.

A Revelation of Grace

I believe that the most-asked question by Christians of their leaders is, "What is God's will?" Isn't that so? There is little confidence in average Christians in their ability or worthiness to hear God for themselves. Dependent and immature. I repeat, the Church is immature and has been for most of its existence. The reason is simply the inability to see the revelation of grace and the finished work of Christ. If the goal is managing sin and keeping it under control, it seems to me we have been failing miserably. Please, let's give ourselves the chance to break out of the religious performance prison and grow up in freedom and liberty.

The more mature one is, the less need for rules. Paul says:

Until we all attain to the unity of the faith, and of the knowledge of the Son of God, to a mature man, to the measure of the stature which belongs to the fullness of Christ. As a result, we are no longer to be children... (Ephesians 4:13-14).

A revelation of grace allows us to mature and motivates us to become someone who is like Jesus. With our focus on behavior and sin management, we cannot eat anything but milk, and thus the nurseries are full of cute but howling babies who cannot feed themselves. After a while, we get on each other's nerves and begin fussing and fighting and making a mess. This scenario sounds like church to me most of the time!

Roy Hessian, a great author and preacher, once asked me, "Little brother, when you preach, do you give the people good advice or good news?" Before I could reply, he continued, "Good advice is not bad, but it won't change their lives. What they need is good news. Even when you are preaching good advice, always end it with good news." That statement began changing the way I taught the Word of God! Good advice is for babies; good news grows them up! The Gospel isn't simply a message of how to be saved, the Gospel is the good news of the finished work of Christ! I am determined to teach all of it, believe all of it, experience all of it, receive all of it, and allow it to transform me into the image of Christ.

Honestly, I think many of us pastors fear our people "growing up"; because if they do, we may not be able to control them! They might develop minds of their own. They might begin questioning the religious drivel and spiritual milk they are being asked to eat each week. The constant rehashing of the same old behaviors—be good boys and girls, do some good works so God will bless, learn to manage your sin, don't tick the Big Guy off—claptrap. Come on, before you throw me under the bus, listen to what is being taught out there in church-land. Are you really listening to this stuff? Most of it is a mixture of law and grace at best. Some of it is just downright religious garbage, but starving folks will eat almost anything.

Now before you jump on pastors, realize that it is really your own fault that some are preaching this message. You end up getting what you want, and milk is what many want. OK, enough of the soapbox. Suffice it to say, legalism in all its forms leads to spiritual immaturity; but a revelation of grace and the finished work of Christ inevitably leads to spiritual maturity and the stature that belongs to the fullness of Christ.

I don't know about you, but I am desperate to see the church grow up and become the world-changing, gates-of-hell-demolishing, love-God-with-all-her-heart entity that Jesus said He was building. That is exactly what grace produces. Allow me to repeat myself, *I am sanctified*, and so are you if you are born again—whether you believe it or not!

Endnote

1. Conform and transform; http://www.merriam-webstercom/dictionary; accessed August 1, 2011.

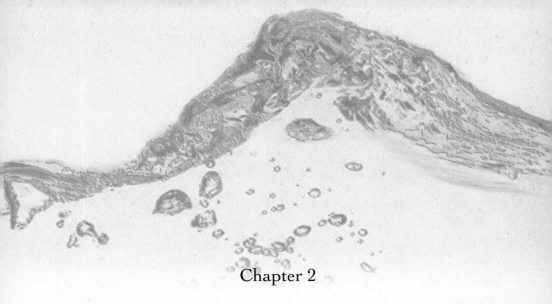

Chapter 2

Receiving the Abundance of Grace

....Those who receive the abundance of grace...
will reign in life.... —Romans 5:17

Do you regularly wake up with a sense of well-being about your-self and your relationship with God? Is there an ongoing sense of awe about being in union with and personally loved by your heavenly Father? When you think about spiritual things and how you are doing in your walk with God, do you judge yourself based on your perfor-mance of a list of ought-to or should-be or will-do? I am attempting to get you to think about focusing on *Jesus'* finished work rather than your unfinished work.

If you are "working" to please Him, you are in for a lifetime of unfinished business, and it will leave you perpetually exhausted!

Let's look at Romans 5:12-17. Paul is contrasting the results of Adam's sin with the results of the righteous life, sacrificial death, and victorious resurrection of Christ. This passage of Scripture sounds very theological and takes some effort to sort through, but it is worth the effort because the bottom line of "getting it" is a dynamically changed life.

> *Therefore, just as through one man [Adam] sin entered into the world, and death through sin, and so death spread to all men, because all sinned—for until the Law sin was in the world; but sin is not imputed when there is no law. Nevertheless death reigned from Adam until Moses, even over those who had not sinned in the likeness of Adam's offense, who is a type of Him who was to come. But the free gift is not like the transgression. For if by the transgression of the one the many died, much more did the grace of God and the **gift by the grace** of the one Man, Jesus Christ, abound to the many. The gift is not like that which came through the one who sinned; for on the one hand the judgment arose from one transgression resulting in condemnation, but on the other hand the free gift arose from many transgressions resulting in justification. For if by the transgression of the one, death reigned through the one, much more those who **receive the abundance of grace** and of the gift of righteousness **will reign in life** through the One, Jesus Christ* (Romans 5:12-17).

Paul makes this astounding statement—he says we can reign in life! Even better, he says we *will* reign in life. I'm not sure what that means exactly, but I want to find out! Don't you like the sound of that?

Reigning in life beats being rained on by life, which is the state of affairs for most of us. We can reign. Many statements in the Word lead me to think this is the way it should be: We are conquerors—more than conquerors—through Christ who loves us (see Rom. 8:37). We can do all things through Christ who strengthens us (see Phil. 4:13). These phrases and others throughout the Bible are inspiring, but not the norm for us to feel and believe most of the time. We have moments when we seem to reign in life, but they fade quickly as the circumstances of life beat us down.

OK, so how do I get there and stay there—reigning in life? Most would set out a plan of action that would go something like this. I'll bet reigners in life pray a lot, read the Bible every day, and do the disciplines that produce a result; therefore, I'll make a plan to do these things and commitment myself for the time it takes to accomplish my goal.

And it may seem to work—for a little while. Then it is back to survival mode again. That is so sad. I have been there many times myself. Our hearts are right, and our motives are pure. We want to "reign in life" for ourselves and for the Kingdom, but we failed again and must look to a new inspiration elsewhere. I hope it comes along soon because I'm dying here! Maybe a new set of CDs or... Won't work, wrong approach. What we have failed to understand is that we don't reign in life through our performance. We reign through our *position!* Not through understanding what to do, but understanding who we are. Those who receive the abundance of grace are the ones who reign in life. Good receivers, not good performers, are the ones who reign!

Romans 6:14 says, *"Sin shall not be master over you, for you are not under law but under grace."* It is not by law-keeping or disciplining our flesh that we overcome sin, experience an abundant life, or achieve any spiritual victory. It all begins with receiving the abundance of grace! Most of us have been taught to be good givers, but few have been taught to be good receivers. Our willingness and sense of liberty to receive all Jesus died to give is the key here!

The fear that pervades the minds of many is that if we preach grace, people will "presume" upon God's grace and use it as an occasion to sin. That opinion comes from a "sin management" mentality and fails to trust the process God designed to conform us to the image of Jesus. We are warned not to sin against grace. Listen, the only way to sin against grace is to refuse to receive the grace it cost Jesus His life to give. Our only hope of *"putting to death the deeds of the body* [flesh]*"* (Rom. 8:13) is receiving the abundance of grace.

Martin Lloyd Jones, a great English preacher and author in the early part of the last century, said, "When you preach grace, unless your conscience accuses you of license you haven't preached grace." My experience proves to me that he is correct! When you extend to yourself and to others the magnitude of grace the Word of God extends, your own conscience will accuse you of licentiousness. You know that if you keep preaching this stuff, your people will begin acting like heathens again! What they need is a clearly defined set of rules and standards of behavior, not greasy grace! As I have said previously, that term offends me at a level beyond my ability to define, and I believe it is offensive to our heavenly Father.

I believe that the Church, in general terms, is mean, prideful, judgmental, and severely unhappy. We are unloving toward our own and viewed by outsiders as graceless and unkind. I think we are this way because we cannot give away what we don't have. We aren't graceful because we haven't received the abundance of grace. We aren't loving because we haven't received the Father's love. We don't love ourselves, and we struggle to love each other because God's great love is an abstract concept that applies only to salvation. If He loves us, He certainly doesn't like us most of the time!

When we are able to receive the *"riches of His grace, which He lavished on us"* (Eph. 1:7-8), and *"the surpassing riches of His grace in kindness toward us in Christ Jesus"* (Eph. 2:7), we will feel rich in grace too! It is easy to give when you are rich. We become gracious and graceful toward ourselves and one another. God is rich in grace, and He has lavished it upon us! *Receive the abundance of grace!* Think about it this way: Mercy paid my debt—then grace made me rich!

Apostle John gives us this statement about Jesus in John 1:14:

And the Word became flesh, and dwelt among us, and we saw His glory, glory as of the only begotten from the Father, full of grace and truth.

The Greek word translated glory is *doxa*. It means, "what one is famous for," "one's renown," "the manifested character of a person."[1] So, a person's glory defines the person, sums up the nature of the person, or shows forth the essence of a person.

When John saw the "essence" of Jesus, he saw two things—*grace and truth*. Jesus was full of grace and truth! (See John 1:14, 17.) Religionists would say, "See there, grace must be balanced with truth." Grace being the mercy side of God and truth the justice or judgment side of God.

There are a couple of big problems I see in this religious view of Jesus:

1. If I am in Christ, I will not face judgment. Christ was judged when He bore my sins on the cross. He was judged to be a sinner for my sake. What most call balance, Paul called mixture, *"a little leaven leavens the whole lump of dough"* (Gal. 5:9).

2. The word translated "truth" in John 1:14 comes from the Greek word *alethinos*, which means "real" or "reality." John isn't talking about judgment or justice or balancing out grace with truth. Jesus came to show us the reality of the invisible world; to show us how things really are in the eternal, invisible world. Jesus is the real, "true Light" (see John 1:9); Jesus is the real, "true Bread" (see John 6:32); Jesus is the real, "true Vine" (see John 15:1). Jesus is *"the Way, and the Truth [reality], and the Life"* (John 14:6). The reality of the matter is that Jesus is full of grace! The truth is that Jesus is full of grace! When John and the others beheld Jesus, they saw one thing— *grace.* He is full of grace!

When the revelation of that truth is fully opened to you and you receive it, you can reign in every area of your life. Good receivers are the ones who reign, good performers have no chance. Religion tells you to perform; the true Gospel instructs you to receive by faith the magnificent finished work of Christ on your behalf. Jesus did not die to make your life on earth harder and more complicated. He died to take your burdens upon Himself so you can be free.

Come to Me, all who are weary and heavy-laden, and I will give you rest. Take My yoke [not religion's yoke] upon you, and learn from Me, for I am gentle and humble in heart; and you will find rest for your souls. For My yoke is easy, and My burden is light (Matthew 11:28-30).

It was for freedom that Christ set us free; therefore keep standing firm and do not be subject again to a yoke of slavery (Galatians 5:1).

There is an abundance of grace waiting to be received that enables us to reign in life.

John 1:16 says, *"For of His fullness we have all received and grace upon grace."* A better translation would be *grace instead of grace* rather than *"grace upon grace."* God's grace is never diminished by my freely receiving what He offers. There is an unlimited amount of it. There is always more of what we received. *Always!* And it is new all the time. Grace instead of grace. Ephesians 2:7 refers to "the surpassing riches of His grace." God is rich in grace, and He is full of grace; and that means there is more of it than we can ever imagine! Never for a moment think it will ever run dry or be less than abundant. Remember, good receivers, not good performers, reign in life.

Now, let's look at the second part of the statement Paul makes in Romans 5:17 as he refers to our ability to reign in life. And I stress again, it is those who receive the abundance of grace and the gift of righteousness who will reign.

ENDNOTE

1. http://strongsnumbers.com/greek/1391.htm; accessed August 1, 2011.

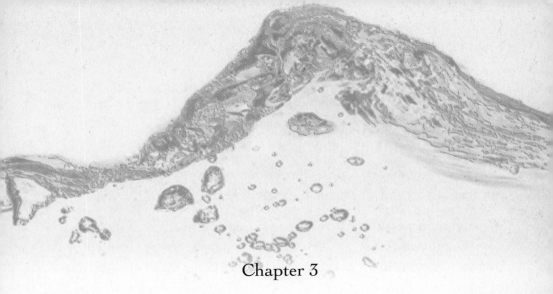

Chapter 3

Receiving the Gift of Righteousness

*...Those who receive the abundance of grace
and of the gift of righteousness will reign in life....*
—Romans 5:17

Have you ever noticed that everything we get from God must be received by faith? For example, the gift of salvation must be received by faith. *"But as many as received Him, to them He gave the right to become children of God"* (John 1:12). John 20:22 gives us a similar statement concerning the Holy Spirit, *"He breathed on them, and said to them, 'Receive the Holy Spirit.'"* It is even possible for us to be in possession of a gift and have never fully received it. It's like having a gift and never opening it! We can also refuse any gift God desires to give. He will not force it upon us nor threaten us if we refuse it.

He will, however, wait us out until our misery factor rises above our fear factor, and we decide to receive by faith!

Righteousness is a gift; and, as is the case with all of God's gifts, it must be fully and wholly received by faith in order to have its intended impact upon our lives. It is my opinion that this subject of righteousness and our understanding of it is the real tipping point for a life lived in freedom and spiritual abundance. It seems that if one receives the gift of righteousness and wholeheartedly embraces the truth of it, all the other points of truth associated with God's great and magnificent plan of grace fall into place.

My personal experience and the testimony of my family, friends, and church members seem to bear that out. Remember, righteousness is a gift to be received, not a goal to be achieved. Christ achieved it, and I receive it! It is done by Him and offered to me. I cannot attain righteousness on my own. I cannot make myself righteous. I am righteous; but I didn't do it, *He did!* It is of highest importance that we understand that the term righteous means right standing. Obviously I am referring to right standing with God.

Righteousness is a state of being. I stand before God righteous, or right with Him, based on who I am, not what I have done or will do. It is a positional reality, not a performance reality. One is either righteous—in right standing with God—or unrighteous. There are only two categories of people on the planet—righteous or unrighteous. There are no gray areas concerning righteousness, no percentages of righteousness. You either are or you are not. You have either received the gift of righteousness or you have not.

I am right with God. I am in a state of being right with God. Jesus did it for me and presented it to me as a gift, and I received it with great gratitude. What a magnificent gift!

> *That if you confess with your mouth Jesus as Lord, and believe in your heart that God raised Him from the dead, you shall be saved; for with the heart a person believes, resulting in **righteousness**...* (Romans 10:9-10).

That is a permanent, Christ-earned state of being that will never change. I am as righteous at this moment as I will be in Heaven! I believe in my heart that God raised Jesus from the dead and confess with my mouth Jesus as Lord, resulting in righteousness.

"He made Him who knew no sin to be sin on our behalf, so that we might become the righteousness of God in Him" (2 Cor. 5:21). I am as righteous as Jesus! I am in right standing with God. I cannot be more "right" with God than the blood of Christ has made me.

Righteous people do righteous deeds, but righteous deeds do not make people righteous! There is only one path to righteousness and that is through faith in Christ's finished work. The apostle Paul alluded to this reality in revealing that the tragedy of the Jewish people was that they were going about trying to establish a righteousness based on law-keeping. I can reign in life by receiving this great gift of righteousness and knowing I have been made righteous because I believe, not because I act right.

Let me ask a question. Can a righteous person do an unrighteous deed? Absolutely, no doubt about it! Does the unrighteous deed that the righteous person did make him unrighteous? *No.* Absolutely not. Why? Righteousness is not based on deeds of any kind, but on faith. Can an unrighteous person do a righteous deed? Certainly, many do good or righteous deeds frequently. Does the righteous deed that the unrighteous person did make the unrighteous person righteous? *No!* Again, there is only one way to become righteous and that is through receiving Christ's gift of righteousness by faith. Righteousness is a state of being; it is not deed-oriented. Righteous is who I am—not what I do. The behavior bar is extremely high to become righteous enough to live in union with God.

Nothing less than sinless perfection is required, and Jesus is the only One who achieved that status. If you are a true Christian, a believer in Christ, one who has been born again, you are righteous, you are in right standing with God, and absolutely nothing can change that. You are as righteous as Christ is righteous.

RIGHT STANDING

Let me tell you a story based on fact, but still fictional. Under the Old Covenant, each head of household in Israel was required each year at Passover to bring a lamb to the priests in Jerusalem as a sacrifice to atone for sins. Thousands of lambs were sacrificed in the city each year. The man would go out into his flock and select a lamb and keep it penned up for four days to examine it for any flaws. Only the best lambs were sacrificed. The man would then head for the city, and for some it was a long journey. The man leading his little lamb came ultimately to the outskirts of Jerusalem where, for the first time, he saw the teeming crowds of people gathered there for Passover.

Immediately he becomes self-aware. Aware of his physical condition after traveling so far, he notices his clothing is threadbare and dirty, his body unbathed and unkempt. This thought crosses his mind, *I hope no one notices how I look, because frankly I'm a mess. Oh well, nothing to do about it now. I'll just have to press on and hope no one notices.* Can you imagine the man thinking such thoughts as he headed for the Temple leading his lamb? I can. I probably would have thought the same thing had I been him. But his worry is misplaced. See, the truth is no one will pay the slightest attention to him. Why? Because all eyes are on the lamb! Everyone, including the priest, will be looking at the lamb, not the man. The lamb is the point of this whole exercise, not the man.

He then hands his lamb over to the priest, and the priest pens up the lamb for four days to again examine it for flaws—only perfect lambs are sacrificed. The priest examines the lamb, not the man!

At the end of the time, the priest makes a pronouncement, "I find no fault in it!" Not only Pontius Pilate, but all of Heaven has said that about your Lamb and mine! "I find no fault in Him!" (See Luke 23:4.)

"Behold, the Lamb of God who takes away the sin of the world," John says in John 1:29. First Peter 1:18-19 says that we are not redeemed with corruptible things such as silver and gold, but by the precious blood of the Lamb. It isn't and never has been about us—it's all about Him! All eyes are still on the Lamb. Read John's marvelous description of our Lamb and what He has accomplished for all of us who believe:

> *And I saw between the throne (with the four living creatures) and the elders a Lamb standing, as if slain, having seven horns and seven eyes, which are the seven Spirits of God, sent out into all the earth. And He came and took the book out of the right hand of Him who sat on the throne. When He had taken the book, the four living creatures and the twenty-four elders fell down before the Lamb, each one holding a harp and golden bowls full of incense, which are the prayers of the saints. And they sang a new song, saying,* **"Worthy are You to take the book and to break its seals; for You were slain, and purchased for God with Your blood men from**

every tribe and tongue and people and nation. You have made them to be a kingdom and priests to our God; and they will reign upon the earth" (Revelation 5:6-10).

My name is in that book and it is sealed. So is yours if you believe! We are as righteous as He is righteous. Our future of reigning that John reveals is a present reality. We don't have to wait until then! We are as righteous now as we will be then. It is finished!

"By this, love is perfected with us, so that we may have confidence in the day of judgment; because as He is, so also are we in this world" (1 John 4:17). As He is so also am I at this present time and forever! If you have believed, you are righteous. If you will receive this great gift, you are on your way to reigning in life and experiencing a never-ending awe at the great grace of our God.

COVERED OR CLEANSED

There is a tragic flaw in the thinking of most believers as they consider themselves and their relationship with God. Most still see themselves as sinners who have been saved by grace. I have discussed this in a previous chapter, but I want to revisit the subject from a different perspective. Most see themselves as sinners, even though they are born again, because they still sin. We all do. Remember, a saint can sin, but the sin does not make the saint a sinner.

A common teaching goes something like this: God is holy, and therefore He cannot associate with sinners such as us. In order to fellowship with us, He put in place a filter between us—the perfect, spotless blood of His own Son. He covered us with Jesus' blood. When God looks at us, He doesn't see the real us, but the us as we appear through the filter of Jesus' blood. When God looks at us, He sees Jesus, not us. If God ever allowed Himself to see us as we really are, we would be toast!

God is covering the real, sinful us with Jesus' blood in order to have a relationship with us, but it is really Jesus in us He is relating to.

Our theology, our songs, and our conversations reveal this "covered by the blood" understanding of what happened when we were saved. It's as if we must have some fine print at the bottom of our contract with God to explain our sinful behavior. This flaw in our theology robs us of the free and joyous intimacy with our great and gracious God that Jesus died to provide.

I find myself cringing every time I hear the phrase spoken by preachers or lyrics in a worship song that use the phrase "covered by the blood." Listen closely. Blood covering is an Old Covenant concept and reality. The blood of sacrificial animals atoned for, or covered, their sins but did not remove their sins. Hebrews 10:11 says, *"Every priest stands daily ministering and offering time after time the same sacrifices, which can never take away sins."* Their sins were covered, but the people were not cleansed. Jesus' sacrifice was not like the sacrifices in the Old Covenant. *"For by one offering He has perfected for all time those who are sanctified"* (Heb. 10:14). *"He [Jesus] has been manifested to put away sin by the sacrifice of Himself"* (Heb. 9:26).

Jesus' blood cleansed me of my sin! That is what enables me to be righteous, or in right standing, with God. *"and the blood of Jesus His Son cleanses us from all sin"* (1 John 1:7). Peter, speaking of the Gentiles who received Christ, says, *"and He made no distinction between us and them, cleansing their hearts by faith"* (Acts 15:9). There is no filter or film of blood between God and me. When God looks at me, He doesn't see me through the blood of Christ, He sees me—cleansed!

Likewise, He sees us as holy and righteous. He sees us, and He loves what He sees! We are God's righteous children, not frauds or hypocrites that He somehow has to fool Himself into fellowshipping with. We are cleansed by the blood of Christ and have become new creatures who belong in God's holy presence.

Remember when Peter was being called to minister to the Gentiles, and in a trance he saw the sheet with all kinds of animals and he was commanded to "kill and eat"? He says, *By no means Lord, for I have never eaten anything unholy and unclean"* (Acts 10:14). Listen to the Lord's reply, *"What God has cleansed, no longer consider unholy"* (Acts 10:15). I want to shout that from the mountaintops! Never consider yourself unholy—you have been cleansed! You are righteous!

We have been blinded to the reality of our heavenly Father's good opinion of us. All of us are so very special to Him. Legalism has taught us to hate ourselves, and that self-hatred has crippled our ability to be the special people He designed us to be and to enjoy His presence as He so fervently desires.

Understanding I am righteous has changed my life.

It will change yours, too.

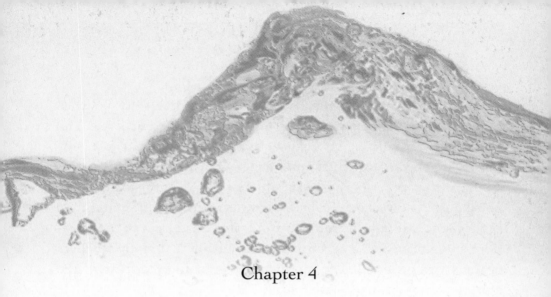

Chapter 4

Are Christians Under the Law?

…The law has jurisdiction over a person as long as he lives.
—Romans 7:1

A person's answer to the question posed in this chapter title will reveal the depth of legalism lodged in that person's thinking. The vast majority of Christians at least hesitate before answering the question: Are Christians under the law? I have asked that question of many thousands of believers over the past 20 years or so. My best guess is that no more than one in 50 immediately and with certainty answers in the negative.

It astounds me that the Body of Christ universally believes the Old Testament Law still has jurisdiction over our lives! The reason it is astounding is because the answer is so clear in Scripture. Few theological questions have such direct and clear answers as this one, yet most Christians seem deeply surprised, if not shocked, at the answer. I see the wheels turning in their minds as they sort through the ramifications of their answer to the question, and always feel a sense of sadness inside that many teachers of the Word have failed so miserably in teaching the truth of the glorious union we have with Christ.

This is a kindergarten question that we miss the answer to almost universally! We should have learned this early on, and our failure to do so has hindered our progress and our ability to tell the story of what Christ has done for us. This is a fundamental truth that we must fully understand or else forever be enslaved to a religious system that produces spiritual death. Some not only give the wrong answer to the question but will argue vehemently against the clear truth presented in Scripture as if they are defending God's honor and the sacredness of His Word. The devil has been at work!

Allow me to pose the question again. Are Christians under the law? *No! No! No!* It is an affront to Christ and His sacrifice of His life to believe otherwise! He died to set you free from the jurisdiction of the law and liberate you from its tyranny. Let's look at Romans 7:1:

> *Or do you not know brethren, (for I am speaking to those who know the law), that the law has jurisdiction over a person as long as he lives?*

In other words, if you see yourself as under the law, you'd better understand it has jurisdiction over you for as long as you live. There is no middle ground here! You are either under the law and will answer to the law in judgment—or under Christ and will answer to Him. Remember His throne is a throne of grace! Jesus or the law, one or the other. Get it?

Paul now gives an illustration of this truth using the Old Testament law concerning marriage.

> *For the married woman is bound by law to her husband while he is living; but if her husband dies, she is released from the law concerning the husband. So then, if while her husband is living she is joined to another man, she shall be called an adulteress; but if her husband dies, she is free from the law, so that she is not an adulteress, though she is joined to another man. Therefore, my brethren, you also were made to die to the Law through the body of Christ, so that you might be joined to another, to Him who was raised from the dead, in order that we might bear fruit for God. For while we were in the flesh, the sinful passions, which were aroused by the Law, were at work in the members of our body to bear fruit for death. But now we have been released from the Law, having died to that by which we were bound, so that we serve in newness of the Spirit and not in oldness of the letter. What shall we say then? Is the Law sin? May it never be! On the contrary, I would not have come to know sin except through the Law; for I would not have known about coveting if the Law had not said, "You shall not covet." But sin, taking opportunity through the commandment, produced in me coveting of every kind; for apart from the Law sin is dead* (Romans 7:2-8).

Are Christians under the law? *No!* He clearly says *no!*

Let me give you an example. Humankind was married to the law. We were all under the jurisdiction of the law at one time. The nature of marriage under the law is for as long as we both shall live. There is no way out, honorably, except if our husband dies; and Jesus said the law will never pass away. So we are married to this "husband" for as long as we both shall live.

The bad news is that this guy is not a very good husband! You won't like him. He is always telling you where you are wrong. You blew it here, and there, and there too. He's always telling you that you are wrong, and he never lifts a finger to help you do what is right. All he does, and can do, is remind you of the standards of behavior and requirements of conduct that are required to stay in right standing in the marriage. He always points out your mistakes but does not have the power or heart to help you do right.

Another infuriating thing about this husband is that he is always right! He knows it, and you know it—and he knows you know. This overbearing, fault-finding, critical, and heartless husband is never going to pass away, which leaves you *trapped, miserable, depressed, and hopeless.* Want to stay there? There is only one honorable way out of this horrible relationship.

All of a sudden, Paul turns this whole thing around and shows us the genius of God and His great grace. While the law will never die, there is another way out. *You* can die! By this time, that option looks attractive, doesn't it? That is exactly what happened when you were born again. Notice Romans 7:4 says, *"you were also were made to die to the Law through the body of Christ, so that you might be joined to another."* And verse 6 says, *"having died to that by which we were bound."* Believers have been released from the law according to Romans 7:6. The word "released" is a military term which means to be discharged. The law no longer has jurisdiction over our lives. What great news! What happened then? We were joined to another, to Him who was raised from the dead.

Romans 6:3-4 says:

*Or do you not know that all of us who have been baptized into Christ Jesus have been baptized into His death? Therefore **we have been buried with Him** through baptism into death, so that as Christ was raised from the dead through the glory of the Father, **so we too might walk in newness of life.***

We came into union with Christ. When that happened, everything changed! We now have the capacity to *"bear fruit for God"* (Rom. 7:4). Under the law we never bore fruit. The law did not have the capacity to impart life, because it was impotent. Jesus imparts life to us, and we bear spiritual fruit.

Galatians 3:21 says, *"…if a law had been given which was able to impart life, then righteousness would indeed have been based on law."* The law cannot impart life. If it could, it would look something like this: Just because it says, "you shall not steal," you immediately stopped stealing and never had that desire again. Or if the law said, "you shall not covet"—BAM—I didn't even notice you had a new Lexus! Not only does the law lack the power to produce righteousness, it actually arouses our sinful passions.

Bearing Fruit

Can we agree that Christians are not under the law? Please consider how very important this elementary truth is to your life and spiritual well-being. Jesus imparts to you the power to bear life-giving fruit as you abide in Him. He says, *"he who abides in Me and I in him, he bears much fruit; for apart from Me you can do nothing"* (John 15:5). A gospel of law-keeping is no gospel at all. There simply is no "good news" associated with a life lived under the law. That is true before salvation and even more applicable after one is saved.

Paul says in Romans 7:24, *"Wretched man that I am! Who will set me free from the body of this death?"* He is referring to his flesh and its total incapacity to keep the law. Then in verse 25 he explodes with dynamic hope because there *is* a way out, *"Thanks be to God through Jesus Christ our Lord!"* Our dying to the law and being joined to Christ is the absolute best news possible.

My observation of people struggling to find peace and joy in their relationship with God over the past thirty-odd years has led me to a conclusion. Most simply do not understand this truth of being released from the law and joined to Jesus. In other words, they do not understand grace! What happens over and over is a moving back and forth between law-keeping and Christ; not in the matter of justification, but in the matter of living out their relationship with God day to day. I see these up and down emotional swings based on how well they perceive they are doing in keeping the list of rules imposed on them. If they feel successful in keeping most of the rules, they feel good about their relationship with God and feel "bless-able." But bad days have the opposite effect. Up and down.

This scenario applies to the ones who haven't given up hope and stayed engaged! Many others simply go through the motions and hope it all works out. *At least we have Heaven to look forward to,* they think, maybe. A common prayer is repeated over and over and reveals a lack of understanding of this simple, fundamental truth we have been discussing. It goes something like this: "God, please help me do better. I'll try harder if You will help me. I know I've failed every day to be the person you want me to be. I'm so sorry. Please forgive me and help me do better." It is difficult to express how heartbreaking it is for me to hear that type of prayer. Jesus did not die to give us that sort of hellish life! Up and down.

Here is a thought I have had for many years. It is not so much that people are up and down, but they are moving from husband to husband! One day they attempt to relate to God through law and rule-keeping; the next day, they relate to God through grace. Moving from husband to husband! In the natural, what is that called? Adultery! Here is the insane thought we have, *I'm going to impress my new husband by having a great relationship with my old one!* I told you it was insane.

Listen closely, please. Jesus, your new Husband, the One you are in spiritual union with, is not impressed with your attempts to please Him through your relationship with the law. He died that you might die with Him and be freed from the tyranny of your flesh stirred up by the law. He desires to impart life to you that you might bear the fruit of the Spirit of God, and your law-keeping mentality is aborting that spiritual process over and over again. Law and grace do not mix!

His throne and His Kingdom are a throne and a Kingdom of *grace*. God is full of grace. Are Christians under the law? *No!* We are in union with Christ; and when that happened, our lives began to be governed by Christ, not by an externally imposed list of laws. We now have an internal allegiance of our spirit to Jesus. When our lives are expressed through our union with Christ, everything He is begins to be released through us. Not law, but love, is the motive of our lives! The inspiration of love becomes the dominant factor of our lives and is able to produce in us what the restraint of law was never able to do.

The greatest constraining power against sin is love, not law! We were designed to abide in Him and bear much fruit. I am not under the law and never will be again. Jesus set me free from the law and gave me a new heart that is capable of loving Him completely and loving my neighbor as myself.

All of the law and the prophets are fulfilled in that great miracle! Jesus says, *"Do not think that I came to abolish the Law or the Prophets; I did not come to abolish but to fulfill"* (Matt. 5:17).

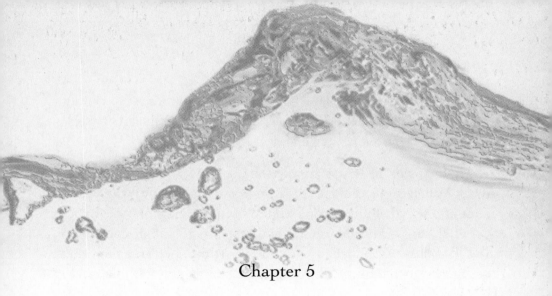

Chapter 5

Two Unchangeable Things

*So that by **two unchangeable things***
in which it is impossible for God to lie....
—Hebrews 6:18

I will never forget a lady in our church responding when I told her I was preaching on Two Unchangeable Things. She immediately said, "I know two unchangeable things; my husband and my big rear end! I can't change either one of them." Those two things weren't what I had in mind, but her response was humorous nonetheless. The two unchangeable things introduced in Hebrews 6 and presented in Hebrews

7-10 are the two pillars upon which the gospel of grace rests. Without these two foundation stones in place, the structure of the Gospel is incomplete and without permanence.

The flip side of that statement is absolutely amazing and life-giving. When one sees these two things and understands the permanence and the absolute completion of them, a sense of security and overwhelming gratitude to God is the result. No other concepts in the Bible show the finished work of Christ more clearly than these two unchangeable things. Let's look at the introductory material in Hebrews 6:

> *For when God made the promise to Abraham, since He could swear by no one greater,* **He swore by Himself, saying "I will surely bless you, and I will multiply you."** *And so, having patiently waited, he obtained the promise. For men swear by one greater than themselves, and with them an oath given as confirmation is an end of every dispute. In the same way God, desiring even more to show to the heirs of the promise the unchangeableness of His purpose, interposed with an oath, so that by two unchangeable things, in which it is impossible for God to lie, we who have taken refuge would have strong encouragement to take hold of the hope set before us. This hope we have as an anchor of the soul, a hope both sure and steadfast and one which enters within the veil, where Jesus has entered as a forerunner for us, having become a high priest forever according to the order of Melchizedek* (Hebrews 6:13-20).

God promised Abraham that He would surely bless him and surely multiply him. This promise was made to Abraham in Genesis 22:16. And Hebrews 6:17 says *"In the same way God, desiring even more to show to the heirs of the promise the unchangeableness of His purpose, interposed with an oath."* God is swearing something to us—the heirs of the promise—just like He swore to Abraham, but even more so. The promise is the same—to bless and multiply us!

God takes an oath on His own name that this promise is true. I believe that the only reason He has come to us is to bless us and multiply us even more so than He did with Abraham! Most of Evangelical Christianity does not present God in such a manner—at least not to other believers. The motive of God to bless is fully extended to those we are presenting the Gospel to without them having to earn it in any way; indeed, we rightfully say they cannot earn it. Then we turn around and require Christians to earn God's blessing. Insane!

It is my observation that many believers have a twisted and distorted view of God as a father. Religion and legalism have painted a portrait of God as a distant, severe, and joyless father figure who is almost impossible to please. They think that meeting with Him is bound to end up with them being rebuked and in need of changing their behavior every time. But Hebrews 6:13 paints a different picture of God. Here He promises and swears an oath that He has come to bless us and multiply us! That is His unchangeable purpose in coming to us.

A great illustration of this reality is the father's joyous reception and eager embracing of his prodigal son in Luke 15. We will look at this parable later when we explore the subject of repentance.

THREE BENEFITS

There are three benefits that come to us through an understanding of these "two unchangeable things in which it is impossible for God to lie."

1. ***Strong encouragement.*** Hebrews 6:18, "*…we who have taken refuge would have strong encouragement to take hold*

of the hope set before us." I don't know about you, but I am frequently in need of encouragement! Most people I know are strongly discouraged more than they are strongly encouraged. Imagine waking up each morning with irrepressible optimism and encouragement about...*everything!* What a way to live. Do you think that living portrait of Christ painted each day by a deeply and permanently encouraged and joyous disciple might be more attractive and irresistible than the distorted and discouraged view of Christ we generally show the world? Where did our joy go? I mean joy in everyday life lived in the world, not just in church on Sundays. I'll tell you where it went. We sacrificed it on the altar of religious activity and rule-keeping that legalism demands. You will never meet a joyous legalist! They simply do not exist. The only joy they get is out of making you miserable! The time has come for Christians to enjoy our relationship with our heavenly Father and celebrate the Good News of a life-changing walk with Him. Let the legalists twist their religious underwear into a wad and be miserable. Don't waste your time dancing to their tunes. Jesus prayed that we might have His joy and that our joy might be full. We need the strong encouragement these two unchangeable things are sure to provide and the accompanying joy that strong encouragement produces.

2. **An anchor for your soul.** Hebrews 6:19, *"This hope we have as an anchor of the soul...."* Our souls represent our mind, will, and emotions. Where we think, decide, and feel. These two unchangeable things will anchor our souls to truth that is life-changing. We won't be tossed

about by every circumstance or incidence that invades our lives. We won't move so easily off our emotional foundations and give in so readily to the storms of life. We can think better, feel better, and choose better when our souls are anchored to these truths. If you want to feel better, you must think better. If you want to act better, you must feel better. You cannot feel badly and act rightly for very long. This anchor for our souls is a huge deal for all believers. The fact that God has taken an oath on His own name to bless us and multiply us should encourage us every day to walk out the rest of our lives feeling good about ourselves and our relationship with Him. Legalism will not allow us to feel good. Grace encourages it!

3. ***A hope that leads us inside the veil.*** Hebrews 6:19, *"...a hope both sure and steadfast and one which enters within the veil."* This is an obvious reference to our living in the presence of God. Our free and total access to God was made certain by Jesus being a forerunner for us as our High Priest (see Heb. 6:20). We belong there, in God's presence, because we are children of God. Our presence is not only welcomed but desired by our heavenly Father, and being in His presence heals us, encourages us, inspires us, and releases in us the power to become who He made us to be. In other words, all we need is provided in His presence. If we get there and stay there, we will be fine.

Do you see God's presence as a place of refuge and hope? Do you feel freely and wholly accepted, and even more, excitedly welcomed by God regardless of your perception of how you are doing with your "to do list"? You should and you can.

We all talk about a need to be intimate with God, but we turn around and present God as one with whom it is almost impossible to be intimate. There is little intimacy with God for most Christians because legalism has distorted our view of what He is like. We say to the lost that God is love, but we don't believe it for ourselves, at least not in the sense that His love translates into His approval of us.

I cannot become intimate with anyone who constantly disapproves of me and requires changes on my part to have fellowship. It is no wonder to me why we must cajole people into having a "quiet time" with God or even consistently reading the Word. Some people's view of God as a disapproving parent and cold enforcer of good behavior destroys any desire for intimacy. None of my family and friends with whom I am intimate treat me that way. Are they more loving than God, my heavenly Father, who loves me with a perfect and everlasting love? Legalism says so.

If you view the Word of God as a rule book or a treatise on how to act to please God, you will not be able to receive from it the life that God designed it to give. A legalistic mindset always reduces the precious revelation of God and His purposes and ways into a condemnatory rule book and reduces you to being a slave.

I don't know about you, but I am sick of religion and am eagerly pursuing the truth about my heavenly Father. He loves me, likes being with me, and delights in spending time with me. I feel the same way about Him! He is my Father and my Friend. These two unchangeable things provide a hope that leads me behind the veil into the glorious presence of God. His throne has become a throne of grace for me. God is the most gracious entity in existence, and He loves me as much as He loves His only begotten Son.

The First Unchangeable Thing

1. Jesus has become our High Priest.

The Latin word for priest is *pontifex,* which means a bridge-build-er.[1] The priest is a man whose function was to build a bridge between man and God. Under the Old Covenant, this was done by means of the sacrificial system which was administered by a tribe of priests led by the high priest. The priesthood was a concession to the fact that men could not and did not keep the Old Testament law perfectly.

Here is an interesting and dynamic truth concerning all of us who are no longer under the law but under grace: *"For when the priesthood is changed, of necessity there takes place a change of law also"* (Heb. 7:12). When Jesus became our High Priest, the law had to change too! We live under the law of love or *"the law of the Spirit of life in Christ Jesus"* as Paul says in Romans 8:2. The Old Testament law is not our law any more. The very fact that a new priesthood has been given shows that the old priesthood was inadequate. According to the law, all priests must belong to the tribe of Levi; but Jesus is from the tribe of Judah. This shows that the whole system of Old Testament law and priesthood is superseded. The law is wiped out as a means of our relating to God. Something greater than the law has come!

Several important facts about Jesus' high priestly ministry need to be remembered:

> A. His priesthood is permanent (see Heb. 7:22-24). Under the old system, the priests died and had to be replaced. There was no permanency; but now there has come a priest who lives forever. Hebrews 7:24, *"but Jesus, on the other hand, because He continues forever, holds His priesthood permanently."* What Jesus is doing as my High Priest, He will continue to do

without interruption forever! Examine Hebrews 7:25, *"Therefore He is able also to save forever those who draw near to God through Him, since He always lives to make intercession for them."* Since He lives forever, He is able to save us forever because He forever is interceding for us! What a magnificent High Priest!

B. Jesus' priesthood is introduced by an oath of God. Psalm 110:4 says, *"The Lord has sworn and will not change His mind, 'You are a priest forever according to the order of Melchizedek.'"* Clearly God does not swear lightly. He never introduced the ordinary priesthood in such a manner. This is something new and so much better that it is almost beyond description.

C. Jesus' priesthood is perfect. He offers no sacrifice for Himself because He is sinless (see Heb. 7:27). He made the one perfect Sacrifice that never needs to be made again, because it has forever opened the way to the presence of God. The function of the priest is to open the door of access to God; once for all Jesus did that, achieving forever what the ordinary and the earthly priesthood could never do. I cannot offer anything that adds to Jesus' sacrifice—not now and not ever. If He lives forever, I am secure forever regardless of what I do or don't do.

Jesus' high priestly ministry did something else that legalists don't get. This new priesthood that ministers the law of love includes you and me! We, as believers, have become a nation of priests, a race of priests, and a royal priesthood. We are also bridge-builders to God— not in the sense that Jesus is, but priests nonetheless. Peter says:

But you are a chosen race, a royal priesthood, a holy nation, a people for God's own possession so that you may proclaim the excellencies of Him who has call you out of darkness into His marvelous light (1 Peter 2:9).

We are bridge-builders to God by the act of proclaiming the "excellencies" of Christ! We all have access to God provided by Christ our High Priest in the same measure that He does! There is no "cleaning ourselves up" before we enter His presence or come before His throne. Jesus has already "cleaned us up" to the point of perfection. Nothing we can do will add anything to that finished work. This Good News reveals the "excellencies" of Christ and is much more attractive than the gospel of behavior modification that legalists proclaim.

Some might ask, "What happens to me when I blow it, when I sin?" Don't you understand He knew you would blow it and sin, and that is precisely why He is our High Priest forever—24/7/365 for eternity! My access to God is based on this unchangeable thing: Jesus is my High Priest; and access to my heavenly Father is the whole ball of wax for me. Nothing is more important than that! His presence does for me and in me everything that needs doing.

In Your presence is fullness of joy; in Your right hand there are pleasures forever (Psalm 16:11).

Now to Him who is able to keep you from stumbling, and to make you stand in the presence of His glory blameless with great joy, to the only God our Savior, through Jesus Christ our Lord, be glory, majesty, dominion and authority, before all time and now and forever. Amen (Jude 24-25).

THE SECOND UNCHANGEABLE THING

2. The New Covenant

It would take a whole book to thoroughly cover the New Covenant. I will do my best to summarize and apply the main points of this remarkable truth to our lives. Remember, this unchangeable thing is a pillar in the foundation of the gospel of grace, and therefore deserves further study.

The New Covenant is unchangeable because it is a covenant, or contract, that has been enacted and completed between God the Father and His only begotten Son, Jesus. All of it was done for me and you! Each of us is so intrinsically valuable and precious to Him that He willingly, and I believe with great joy, emptied Himself of His Godhead, became a human being, resisted the temptations of satan, lived a perfect life, took our sins upon Himself, endured an horrific death, and fulfilled every requirement of the law to make sure nothing about our redemption was left for us to perform. We still have little understanding of what price He paid to secure for us this glorious and magnificent covenant. It is an understatement of gigantic proportions simply to say, *"He is also the Mediator of a better covenant, which has been enacted on better promises"* (Heb. 8:6).

The writer of Hebrews, or anyone else for that matter, did not have the capacity to express how much better the promises of the New Covenant are to us! This New Covenant is almost beyond belief, and is so good and thorough that many stumble over its promises and won't allow themselves to receive the full measure of its provisions. Listen, it is not an act of humility, or honoring to God, to ever refuse to believe or receive anything Jesus died to give. He died to give us all the benefits and blessings of this perfectly performed and executed covenant. We must never allow religionists and legalists to tag on addendums of human performance to this divine contract.

The Judaizers tried it with Paul, and his reaction was almost violent! Read Paul's words as he confronts the Galatians who have been duped by the legalists into believing the New Covenant needed some fine print added to it.

> *But now that you have come to know God, or rather to be known by God, how is it that you turn back again to the weak and worthless elemental things, to which you desire to be enslaved all over again? You observe days and months and seasons and years. I fear for you, that perhaps I have labored over you in vain* (Galatians 4:9-11).

Any attempt to add human performance to the New Covenant must always be confronted aggressively and resisted with determination. I believe legalists have a poor understanding of the New Covenant. Modern legalists defend the New Covenant and the finished work of Christ as it pertains to justification—salvation—but always add to it with performance rules and requirements for sanctification; the old "saved by grace but perfected by the flesh" concept of the New Covenant. Enough of this religious junk! It is utterly wrong and calls into question the efficacy of Jesus' sacrifice. Pastors and teachers must stop trying to "help" Jesus by keeping His people under their religious control. We simply are not their High Priest—He is! We must stop adding to the New Covenant and trust Christ as His people's High Priest.

There are some who think of themselves as priestly caretakers of God's children, but Jesus is the only High Priest. We don't have either right nor authority to add our fleshly requirements and idiotic rules to the gloriously designed and perfectly performed covenant Jesus shed

His blood to provide for all of us. Some may think they are doing a great service to God's people, but they need to think again. They are, in actuality, performing a great service for the enemies of Christ and His people. Bottom line—the New Covenant is perfect as it is.

Let's look at what happened when the New Covenant was ratified. Hebrews 10:9 says, *"Then He said, 'Behold I have come to do Your will.' He takes away the first in order to establish the second."* Jesus came to do the will of God, and He did the will of God perfectly and absolutely when He came. He kept every aspect of the law perfectly. He never sinned. He did not come to destroy the law but to fulfill it (see Matt. 5:17-18). He "filled to the full" the requirements of the law. He satisfied the law. By doing the will of God, He took away the first covenant in order to establish the second covenant.

> *By this will we have been sanctified through the offering of the body of Jesus Christ once for all. Every priest stands daily ministering and offering time after time the same sacrifices, which can never take away sins; but He, having offered one sacrifice for sins for all time, sat down at the right hand of God, waiting from that time onward until His enemies be made a footstool for His feet. For by one offering He has perfected for all time those who are sanctified* (Hebrews 10:10-14).

By Jesus' performance of the will of God, we have been sanctified through the offering of the Body of Jesus Christ once for all. *Amazing!* Jesus could offer Himself as a perfect Sacrifice because He was perfect; and in doing that, we who believe have been perfected too! Sanctified means having been made perfect. That doesn't mean I cannot sin, but it does mean I cannot become a sinner. Sin is confined to the flesh now, and sin is not laid to my account!

Jesus has perfected for all time those who have been made perfect. Please don't argue with God about this. Don't allow the enemy and his agents to move you off this glorious truth regardless of how hard it is to believe. If you will accept the reality that you are fully sanctified and wholly acceptable to God without sin attached to you, a remarkable thing will slowly begin to happen. You begin to be transformed through the renewing of your mind into the image of God. Love begins to govern your life, love for God, love for yourself, and love for others. You begin to become who you were created to be. That is the power of the New Covenant at work in you.

Our union with Christ and our free access to our heavenly Father begins to produce the fruit of the Holy Spirit in us. The New Covenant guarantees that God's throne is a throne of grace and as we access His presence and continue to abide there, we are transformed into His image. If we will continue to "see" Him, we will become like Him. Human effort through law-keeping will not produce Christ-likeness. The New Covenant will.

A New Covenant Illustration

Imagine a scene with me: God comes to the nation of Israel and says, "I want to make a deal with you, a covenant with you. Understand that all covenants are conditional. They are conditioned upon the performance of both parties in fulfilling their promises. I do My part and you do your part, and we have an ongoing deal. OK?"

Now, God says, "Here's My part of the covenant and My promises. I am going to bless you and multiply you. I will be your God and you will be My special people. All of your needs will be met— physical, emotional, and spiritual. Your clothes will not wear out, your crops will grow and produce, your animals will be healthy, you will never be sick, no enemies will defeat you, and you will prosper in everything you touch. (Read Deuteronomy—amazing promises). All right, that is my part of the covenant. Your part is to keep My law in every respect. If you break it in any way, the covenant is nullified. I will do My part and you do your part, and we have a deal."

The nation of Israel stuck out their hand to shake on the deal and said, "OK, sweet, that sounds good to us."

They shake hands with God with great expectations. They had no idea they could not do it, but they soon learned the impossibility of perfect performance by human flesh. God knew it was impossible for them, though, and that is precisely why almost simultaneously He instituted the priesthood and the sacrificial system. This is what most of the Old Testament is about, really. Israel running away from God, and God pursuing them; then coming back and being blessed, then jumping the tracks again, and God pursuing. They couldn't do it, and neither can we!

Then in the fullness of God's time, He comes to His people, including the Gentiles this time, (better promises!) and says, "I want to make a new covenant with you. The old one isn't working out very well and we need a change. I'm going to base this covenant on some better promises, and I'm confident the results will be much better. My part is essentially the same as before. I will bless and multiply you, I'll be your God and you will be My people (family). I will provide for you, bless you, love you, and you will have life and life abundant. [If you see the physical promises in the old as types of spiritual realities in the new, you will see the parallels.] That is My part and My promises. Now, let's talk about your part. You must agree that you didn't do so well with your part last time, right?

"I will tell you what I am going to do. I have decided to up My end of the bargain quite significantly. I think you will agree that it is a better deal for you. I am going to do My part—and I am going to do your part too! Allow Me to repeat myself, I am going to do My part, and I am going to do your part, too!"

God shook hands with His own dear Son and the New Covenant was ratified. That is as secure as any conditional covenant can ever be! God did His part…and our part too, since we could not do it. Jesus kept the law and fulfilled its requirements for us. He did for me what I could not do for myself! This New Covenant is between God and His dear Son. Our part is to believe and receive what Jesus died to give.

Believe and receive this finished work of Christ and the blessing of a loving Father. That is all we have to do. That is all we can do. These two unchangeable things, Jesus becoming our High Priest forever and the New Covenant He mediated for us, provide strong encouragement, an anchor for our souls, and a hope that leads us into God's presence where we can become who we have already been made to be.

See, the Gospel really is Good News, isn't it?

ENDNOTE

1. http://dictionary.reference.com/browse/pontifex; accessed August 3, 2011.

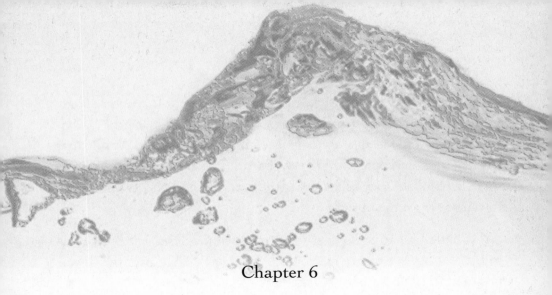

Chapter 6

Where on Earth Does God Live?

I have surely built You a lofty house,
a place for Your dwelling forever.
—1 Kings 8:13

When our two daughters were children, they each were born again. From the time they were old enough to communicate, they heard the Gospel spoken through Martha, my wife, and me, other teachers, leaders, and friends in our church. After they had received Christ, I clearly remember asking each of them this question: "Where does Jesus live now?" They both responded without any coaching, "He lives in my heart." While that response was without full understanding, it was, in broad terms, theologically accurate. Their little bodies had become the *"temple of the Holy Spirit"* (1 Cor. 6:19). While that supernatural and spiritual rebirth did not feel all that remarkable to them at the time, they each have come to realize and deeply appreciate the enormity of the miracle.

What God had to do in each of us who know Him was prepare us to become a place where He could live forever. That, my friend, was no small feat! God in me? Amazing!

There is a pattern in Scripture repeated all the way through that establishes a dynamic and life-affecting truth concerning God's dwelling places or "houses" on earth. The dramatic conclusion one can draw from this truth is simple to be sure, but nonetheless powerful because of its simplicity. When I saw it one day, it made me weep with gratitude and then shout for joy. It is not complicated, but boy is it good! We will draw this conclusion together, concerning us being God's house, at the end of this chapter. There will be hints of this truth all the way through, so stay with me.

GOD'S DWELLING PLACES ON EARTH

There are four houses, a synonym for dwelling places, that God has occupied in biblical history. I am listing them for our study this way:

1. God's Primary House

2. God's Pattern House

3. God's Perfect House

4. God's Permanent House

Each was a house that was designed, desecrated, desolated, and destroyed.

As we begin our study, it is of paramount importance that you understand God will not live in a dirty house. He, being the holy God that He is, cannot accommodate sin in His presence. Let me repeat, God will not live in a dirty house!

I heard the story of a group of fraternity boys who had a billy goat as their mascot at fraternity competitions. When they ran short of money, they thought of selling the goat because they couldn't afford to board it at the farm. During a discussion, one of the boys volunteered to keep the goat in his room at the frat house. His girlfriend immediately said, "What about the smell?" The boy looked around at his friends and replied, "Oh, don't worry about the smell, I'm sure the goat will get used to it pretty fast!" College boys are more than willing to live in a dirty room, but God will not live in a dirty house. Now, let's look at the houses in which God has lived on earth.

1. God's Primary House—Adam

Adam was a house designed. Genesis 2:7 says, *"Then the Lord God formed man of dust from the ground, and breathed into his nostrils the breath of life; and man became a living being."* God designed a house of three rooms. Adam was fashioned body, soul, and spirit. God formed from the dust of the ground man's body. God then breathed into his nostrils the breath or Spirit of life. Adam then became a living being or soul—body, soul, and spirit.

Paul says in First Thessalonians 5:23:

Now may the God of peace Himself sanctify you entirely; and may your spirit and soul and body be preserved complete, without blame at the coming of our Lord Jesus Christ.

I have a body and know the physical world. I have a soul, or "psyche," and I have psychological life and know the social and psychological world. I have a spirit, and I have spiritual life (if born again). When my body is right, I am healthy. When my soul is right, I am happy. When my spirit is alive (born again), I am holy. Adam had not sinned at this point therefore His spirit was the dwelling place of God. Adam was a house designed.

Adam was a house desecrated. Genesis 3:6 says, *"When the woman saw that the tree was good for food, and that it was a delight to the eyes, and that the tree was desirable to make one wise, she took from its fruit and ate."* Adam desecrated his holy temple with sin.

Adam was a house desolated. God moved out and Adam became lord over his own house. He was without God! Now notice the fourth step.

Adam was a house destroyed. God destroyed His primary house. Genesis 2:17 says, *"…for in the day that you eat from it you will surely die."* Adam died spiritually that day because he was separated from God who is the Giver and Source of life. Death was passed to the whole human race. Adam was a house destroyed. God will not live in a dirty house.

2. God's Pattern House

God's pattern house was the temple. Solomon speaks of the temple in First Kings 8:27, *"But will God indeed dwell on the earth? Behold, heaven and the highest heaven cannot contain You, how much less this house which I have built!"*

The temple was a house designed. It was built on the same pattern as Adam. It was a house of three rooms: outer court—the place of sacrifice, corresponding to the human body; inner court—the place of fellowship, corresponding to the human soul; Holy of Holies—the dwelling place of God, corresponding to the human spirit. God commanded David and Solomon to build it according to *"the pattern"* (Exod. 25:9). The temple was one big and elaborate object lesson! It was never meant to be a permanent dwelling of God.

The temple was a house desecrated. Jesus speaks of the temple during Herod's reign in Matthew 21:13, *"...It is written, 'My house shall be called a house of prayer'; but you are making it a robber's den.'"* God designed it and they desecrated it.

The temple was a house desolated. Matthew 23:38, *"Behold, your house is left to you desolate."* Before, in John 2:16, Jesus says, *"My Father's house,"* but now in Matthew 23:38, He says, *"your house is left to you desolate."* God has left the temple! They still performed all the rituals of worship, but God was gone. God will not live in a dirty house!

The temple was a house destroyed. Matthew 24:2 says, *"...Truly I say to you, not one stone here will be left upon another, which will not be torn down."* And He was right! The temple was utterly destroyed in A.D. 70, never to be rebuilt. God's pattern house was destroyed.

3. God's Perfect House—Jesus

John 2:19-21 says, *"Jesus answered them, 'Destroy this temple and in three days I will raise it up.' The Jews then said, 'It took forty-six years to build this temple, and will You raise it up in three days?' But He was speaking of the temple of His body."*

Jesus was a house designed. He was perfect in body, soul, and spirit.

Jesus was a house desecrated. Second Corinthians 5:21 says, *"He made Him who knew no sin to be sin on our behalf, so that we might become the righteousness of God in Him."* Jesus became a dirty house when He took the sins of the world upon Himself. The perfect Lamb of God was desecrated!

Jesus was a house desolated. Matthew 27:46 says, *"And about the ninth hour Jesus cried out with a loud voice, saying, 'Eli, Eli, Lama Sabachthani?' that is, 'My God, My God, why have You forsaken me?'"* Get this picture in your mind. God moved out of His own Son! Our heavenly Father cannot, will not, accommodate sin in His presence.

Jesus became a house destroyed. Alone, suspended between Heaven and earth, Jesus died. Romans 8:32 says, *"He who did not spare His own Son, but delivered Him over for us all, how will He not also with Him freely give us all things?"* Jesus knew the penalty for sin is death, yet He willingly took my sin, your sin, upon Himself and died that we would live. *"And Jesus cried out again with a loud voice, and yielded up His spirit"* (Matt. 27:50).

4. God's Permanent House—the Body of Christ

Where on earth does God live? His permanent home on earth is the Body of Christ—He lives in you and me. Our daughters, Wendy and Abby, in their childlike response to my question, "Where does Jesus live now?" got it right! He lives in every believer; He lives not a temple made with hands, but a living temple made up of all God's children. Each of us is a living stone in the house of God. We do not enter His house on Sunday, we are His house on Sunday—and on Monday and Tuesday and....

First Corinthians 6:19 says, *"Or do you not know that your body is a temple of the Holy Spirit who is in you, whom you have from God, and that you are not your own?"* And John 14:16-17 says, *"And I will ask the Father and He will give you another Helper, that He may be with you forever; that is the Spirit of Truth, whom the world cannot receive,* because it does not see Him or know Him, but you know Him because He abides with you, and will be in you." Notice the promise, "that He may be with you forever." We are God's permanent house! That is why He could truthfully say, *"I will never desert you, nor will I ever forsake you"* (Heb. 13:5).

A Clean House

Now it is time for the life-changing conclusion to this whole study about where God lives on earth. Remember two facts: God will not live in a dirty house, and you are God's permanent house. The only conclusion reasonable people can come to is this unalterable truth: I am not dirty! Believers are not dirty! My conclusion is biblically backed: Acts 10:15, *"What God has cleansed, no longer consider unholy."* Isaiah 1:18, *"Though your sins are as scarlet, they will be white as snow; though they are red like crimson, they will be like wool."* Hebrews 10:17, *"their sins and their lawless deeds I will remember no more."*

All of us, if we walk in the flesh, have the capacity to do "dirty deeds," but we are not dirty. As this truth begins to renew my mind, I find myself much less prone to deeds of the flesh, and the Spirit of God within coaches and empowers me to put off the deeds of the flesh. I am secure in the finished work of Christ cleansing me of my sins—past, present, and future. It is now Christ in me, my hope of glory (see Col. 1:27).

It makes me happy, knowing I am holy! I am not dirty! I have preached on this topic several times in churches across the country; and when I go back to those places, believers will shout out to me, "Pastor Clark, I'm not dirty!"

While the truth is simple, it will change your life to come into agreement with God about the finished work of Christ on your behalf. God fashioned a house that is perfectly clean, He then moved in and will never leave. Remember what was said in a previous chapter. Salvation is not getting us out of earth into Heaven. Salvation is getting God out of Heaven into us!

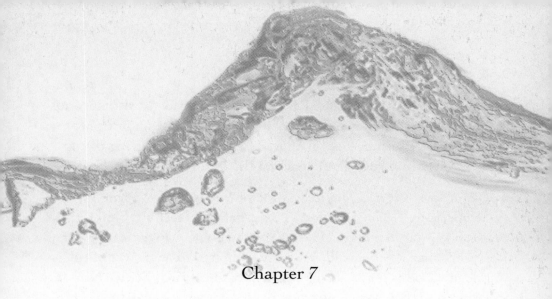

Like Rats in a Maze

If we confess our sins, He is faithful....
—1 John 1:9

From the moment of my birth
To the instant of my death,
There are patterns I must follow
Just as I must breathe each breath.
Like a rat in a maze
The path before me lies,
And the pattern never alters
Until the rat dies.[1]

Religion and legalistic Christianity are tools the enemy uses to limit the damage done to his kingdom by the finished work of Christ. He uses religion to keep people out of the Kingdom of God through the lie of works-based salvation. He uses legalistic Christianity to keep true Christians from being able to demonstrate and display to the world the glorious Gospel of grace, and thereby limiting the impact a transformed life should have on the world.

Paul says, *"It was for freedom that Christ set us free"* not for *"a yoke of slavery"* (Gal. 5:1). Sadly, most believers feel like Simon and Garfunkel's rat in a maze. There seems to be no way out of the performance maze that gets increasingly complicated as the list of rules is added to, or changed at, the whim of the next preacher we hear or book we read. Believers keep trudging along, their heads down, lost in the maze of rules, without much hope of success until they die and go to Heaven. What a grotesque picture of the glorious Gospel!

While what we are about to see in the Word of God may at first be upsetting because of the patterns of thinking that are so deeply imbedded in our minds, please consider that our minds must be renewed from years of believing lies. That renewal process does not happen without some measure of upset!

Are you ready to break out of the maze of legalism and off the treadmill of religion and enter the glorious liberty that Christ's sacrifice on the cross provides? What follows should help you make this transition.

Confession, Repentance, Conviction

There are three concepts of Christian activity that are keys to unlocking the maze or prison of legalism—confession, repentance, and conviction. These three terms represent concepts that are so deeply ingrained in most believers' thinking that they are accepted as truth without question. I am convinced we have believed the enemy's lies about all three and turned these good life-giving gifts into an entryway for bondage.

Confession

The word translated confess comes from the Greek word *homolo-geo*. It means "same word" or to "agree with."[2] There is also the idea of verbally "agreeing with." Here is one problem with the term confess or confession that plagues most believers; confession and sin are always tied together in our minds, and because of that we are limited in our concept of the practice of confession.

When I say "confess" to someone, they invariably think of confessing sin. When I ask, "What do you first need to do to be free from sin?" they invariably say we must confess it. Confess is a great and grand word. To me it means to agree with the Word and verbalize that agreement. So with that in mind, how about confessing: Jesus is Lord; I am the righteousness of God in Christ Jesus; My sins and lawless deeds He has remembered no more; God has removed my sins from me as far as the east is from the west; I am cleansed by the blood of Jesus; God is great and greatly to be praised; or any number of other great truths.

The concept of confession is a truly wonderful and life-giving concept that has been limited to the confession of sin. There is a place in our lives for the confession of sin, but do not limit confession to that single exercise! As much as the practice of confession of sin is talked about and used in our conversations with each other and in our teaching of believers about how to progress in their discipleship, one would think the term is found throughout the New Testament. I mean, it must be found in almost every chapter, wouldn't you think? This commonly held idea—that for a Christian (notice I said *Christian*) to be forgiven, and therefore right with God, he or she must first confess the sin and ask for forgiveness—is so widely embraced and commonly taught that few even question whether the practice is biblical. Contrary to obvious, popular opinion, the term *confess* is found only five times in the New Testament!

1. **Matthew 3:6**—*"And they were being baptized by him in the Jordan River, as they confessed their sins."* (Mark 1:5 is a parallel verse). This reference was clearly under the ministry of John the Baptist and is not referring to New Testament Christians.

2. **Matthew 10:32**—*"Therefore everyone who confesses Me before men, I will also confess him before My Father who is in heaven."* No reference to sin is stated or implied.

3. **Romans 10:9-10**—*"That if you confess with your mouth Jesus as Lord, and believe in your heart that God raised Him from the dead, you will be saved; for with the heart a person believes, resulting in righteousness, and with the mouth he confesses, resulting in salvation."* Again, there is no reference to confession of sin but a confession that Jesus is Lord.

4. **James 5:16**—*"Therefore, confess your sins to one another, and pray for one another, so that you may be healed."* This is the first reference in the New Testament that refers to confession of sin by a believer! We are to confess our sins to one another to be healed. This is a practice that needs to take place among us for healing and will happen much more often as the Church shakes off legalism and begins to walk in grace. There is a liberty, freedom, and sense of security required to be free to confess sin to one another. An atmosphere of love, acceptance, and lack of judgmentalism will promote this healing practice. We can be free from putting on a religious front and become more transparent before God

and each other. Legalistic Christianity will not tolerate such a thing! If you don't believe me, try it and see.

I want to take some additional time with the last reference to confession of sin. It is the only verse in the New Testament that refers to our confessing our sins to God. Isn't that hard to believe? Again, from the way this practice dominates the Church's thinking, one would be led to believe there are hundreds of references. Not so. There is only one verse in the entire New Testament that requires us to confess our sins to God to be forgiven. One! This one verse is the fulcrum verse that tips your life toward legalism or toward grace, toward religion or toward intimacy with God, toward a life of performance or toward a life of rest and security, toward bondage or toward freedom, toward law or toward love.

It is therefore imperative that this verse be accurately interpreted, and it has *not* been. It is the most abused, misinterpreted, and misapplied verse in the whole Bible. Our Catholic friends base a major part of their daily and weekly ritual on a misinterpretation of this verse. Our Protestant friends worldwide base more of their theology than they care to admit on a misinterpretation of this one verse. Christians all around the world and for generations have misinterpreted this verse, and, therefore, have misapplied it and allowed the enemy of our lives to leaven the truth with legalism.

Whenever the subjects of sin and the need of confession are raised, this verse is universally quoted and trotted out as a proof text. Why? Because there aren't any others to quote! The devil is a genius at what he does, and he has accomplished much of his strategy to enslave believers whom Jesus died to set free by leading us to misapply one verse in the Bible. I hear this verse quoted in sermons and Bible studies on a frequent basis, and probably so do you. It has to be demonic how much misery a misinterpretation this wonderful, Holy Spirit-inspired verse has perpetuated. Only John 3:16 is more memorized than this verse. Even the newest of Christians can quote it!

I don't know all of the enemy's strategy behind this lie, but I do know at least part of it. He wants Bible believers, those who really do believe that what the Bible says is true, to misinterpret a verse here and there at critical places, and thereby insert the leaven of the law into our thinking. It doesn't take much because "a little leaven, leavens the whole lump." In this case, the devil has been spectacularly successful! He is so good at his craft that we will sometimes defend our positions even though they are proven to be wrong.

I anticipate such a response from some to what I am about to say concerning First John 1:9. If you want to escape the endless cycle of religiously imposed requirements to be forgiven by God for sin, then listen with your mind fully engaged. If you want to break out of the maze of legalism and begin embracing the liberty that cost Jesus His life to provide, lay down your preconceived beliefs about what God requires of you, and listen to the truth. Allow your mind to be transformed concerning this crucial and life-giving understanding of this one verse.

5. **1 John 1:9**—*"If we confess our sins, He is faithful and righteous to forgive us our sins and to cleanse us from all unrighteousness."* When the subject of how to deal with

sin in the life of a believer is brought up, this verse is always quoted because there aren't any others to quote!

I know I am repeating myself, but it is necessary to drive home this crucial point of truth. New believers are discipled to begin this cycle of confession and forgiveness by God in their spiritual infancy. If you sin, they say, you are not right with God; and in order to get right with God so He can bless and use you, you need to confess your sin to God, and He will forgive you. Some say we need to "keep short sin accounts with God" and stay up to date with our confession so we can be holy enough to be useful to Him.

I always wondered what happened if I forgot some of the sins I should have confessed or sins I didn't even know about—you know, the "sins of omission." I spent a few years on that treadmill going nowhere fast! The harder I tried, the further behind I got. It is a truly horrible way to live and always ends with a hardened heart or senseless pride at the thought of doing better, at least, than some other people I knew.

Believing this lie that so glibly and with such conviction came from those whose spiritual lives I admired almost killed me spiritually. If not for the promise of Heaven and the threat of hell, I would have gladly gone back to the seeming sanity of life without the religious misery. Little of it made sense to me, but I trusted those who knew more than I did. The problem was that what they "knew" was devastatingly wrong! It took me many years to find out for myself what the truth really was. I have been back now for many years and am more excited about my relationship with my heavenly Father than at any point in my life. He, my friend, is a really good Father, and life with Him is glorious beyond description. All right, let's talk about First John 1:9.

First John 1:9

First John 1:9 does not say that a Christian must confess sins to God in order to be forgiven. It does say one must confess sins to God in order to be saved. Big difference! This verse is not directed toward believers, but toward those who need salvation. Read the first eight verses in First John 1 and it will be clear to you that John is showing unbelievers how to be saved. John is saying that the one who we have come to know, the one we have heard, touched, and fellowshipped with, we want you to know Him like we know Him. First John 1:9 tells us how to know Him! *"If we confess our sins, He is faithful and righteous to forgive us our sins and to cleanse us from all unrighteousness."*

In order to be born again, there must be agreement with God about the fact that we are sinners in need of a Savior. Here's the question, Did you confess your sin when you were saved? Yes, you did. You agreed with God about being a sinner, right? If so, was He faithful and was He righteous to forgive your sins? Yes. But He did not stop there. He also was faithful to cleanse you from all unrighteousness. You became righteous. Is there any unrighteousness not included? No! He forgave *all* your sin—past, present, and future. You were cleansed of all unrighteousness and made to be the "righteousness of God in Christ."

Sin can no longer be laid to your account. He didn't just forgive your sins up to the time you were saved, He forgave all your sins forever. You were born again and entered a state of being called *righteousness* or right standing with God. You are not required to confess your sin to God in order to be forgiven ever again. You already are forgiven. You are as forgiven now as you ever will be, even in Heaven.

You may need to confess to be healed, but not to be forgiven. First John 1:9 does not apply to me any longer since I have confessed my sins and have been forgiven. The verse for all of us who are born again concerning what happens when we sin is two verses later in First John 2:1, *"My little children* [see, we are addressed now as children of God], *I am writing these things to you so that you may not sin. And if anyone sins, we have an Advocate with the Father, Jesus Christ the righteous."* He knew we would sin and that is precisely why He is our Advocate with the Father.

As a Christian, I do not confess sin to God in order to be forgiven. I already am forgiven; and furthermore, I am cleansed of sin and have become the righteousness of God in Christ. That does not mean I never interact with God about sin, but it does mean it is a fruitless religious exercise to ask for what has already been given.

Confession is for my healing, not for God's forgiveness. There is no biblical basis to believe otherwise. That doesn't mean I am not sensitive to the Holy Spirit as He reveals areas of my life and thinking that need changing, or that there aren't times for confession or agreement with Him about sin. But it does mean I am not required to ask for or receive further forgiveness. Now please get this in your mind and never forget it.

God has forgiven me of my sins—past sins, present sins, and future sins. There is not a sin that I will ever commit that He has not already forgiven and cleansed. *"Blessed is the man whose sin the Lord will not take into account"* (Rom. 4:8) *"...God was in Christ reconciling the world to Himself, not counting their trespasses against them..."* (2 Cor. 5:19). If Jesus' advocacy for me isn't absolute, I have no hope of intimacy with my heavenly Father, but since it is, my Father's throne is a throne of grace for me forever. I never, never, never, have to crawl into His presence like some sinful, dirty thing. He always welcomes me as a son of whom He is proud and empowers me by His glorious presence to become the person He has already created me to be. See, He knows something the Pharisees among us don't. He knows that if I spend time with Him, I can become like Him!

I absolutely love seeing my children come through my door regardless of their state of mind, and their presence with me is one of the greatest joys of my life. They aren't perfect in living out the life God has given them, but I don't care. As far as I am concerned, they are the best children in the world. I could not be any more proud of them no matter what accomplishments might be in their future. I want to see them, talk to them, and treasure each moment with them because I love them more than my own life. If they want to bring up some struggles they are having, I will listen and try to help; but if they don't, that is fine too. I just enjoy being with them.

Our heavenly Father loves us all infinitely more than I love my children. He doesn't want to hear us beg for the forgiveness that He has already sacrificed His Son to provide and secure for us all. It is finished! Now, let us get on with enjoying our relationship with the Creator of the universe and honoring Him by believing the truth about the finished work of His dear Son.

A good starting place is to believe the truth revealed in First John 1:9 and never again allowing the enemy to enslave us in the legalism that the misapplication of that one verse has produced.

Repentance

Repentance is another concept that has been hijacked by the enemy and distorted in order to keep the sons and daughters of God in bondage to legalism. This good and precious gift has been turned into a hideous caricature of itself and robbed of its power to help liberate us from the power of deception. As with confession, repentance has always been tied to sin like conjoined twins and thereby limited in its intended impact on our lives.

If I were to say to you, "You need to repent," what would you immediately think? After your anger and resistance abated, you would think of some sin of which you need to repent, right? Repentance is viewed as a necessary but onerous requirement in dealing with sin and staying in God's good graces. It is a tool to be used to keep us in line and to prevent us from acting like the heathens we once were. If behavior modification is the goal, and it is with all legalists, then repentance is viewed as the primary method of accomplishing it.

Ongoing repentance is necessary to keep an angry God happy enough with you to be willing to bless you and use you. Your standing with God must be maintained by ongoing good behavior, and the only way to accomplish this behavior standard is through frequent sessions with God where you confess all known sins, ask for forgiveness, and repent or turn away from those sins. This treadmill of religious activity makes logical sense if you adhere to the "saved by grace but perfected by the flesh" deception that legalists teach.

Some preachers and teachers are more kind about it than others and more understanding of the difficulty of changing sinful behavior, but the end result is the same. One earns blessing by being good and displeasure by being bad. Good behavior and the resulting blessing of God are achieved, at least initially, by repentance.

Revivalist's altar calls are almost always geared toward getting the most Christians possible to "repent of their sins" and rededicate their flesh to better behavior resulting in God being happy and changing His mind (repenting!) about punishing the evildoers. This scenario must be repeated over and over again because flesh is incorrigible and cannot be dedicated! That is precisely why this type of revival is worthless—except to keep the preachers employed.

The devil is delighted by all attempts to "perfect the flesh," because he knows it is impossible, and the effort expended in the process leaves us tired and vulnerable to deception. The harder we try, the "behinder" we get! We are traveling in the wrong direction, but we sure are making good time! We may not be accomplishing anything of lasting value, but at least we are making a great effort! Legalistic Christianity keeps us busy, but accomplishes nothing in procuring the great and glorious promise of our Lord: I have come that you might have life and life abundant (see John 10:10).

The guilt and shame that is always associated with repentance causes this great gift to be, almost universally, thought of in a negative light and resisted rather than embraced as it should be and will be when seen correctly. The resulting attitude is that we will do it if we must, but we certainly would rather not! I believe repentance, properly understood, is a pathway to growing up in all aspects into Him and experiencing the transforming and liberating power of truth. Remember, the Truth will set you free! (See John 8:32.)

The word translated repent comes from the Greek work *metanoia*, which means "to perceive afterward" or "after thought" or "to think again" or "rethink."[3] It essentially means to rethink your position in light of truth, or change your mind based on the fact that you thought wrongly before and need to embrace the truth of a matter.

Repentance is a gift from God in that He gave us the ability to receive truth, and that truth then transforms our minds. When our minds are changed or conformed to the truth on any matter or situation, we begin to think as He thinks. For example, have you ever thought that something was impossible? Of course, we all have had that thought. Do you think God has ever had that thought? Absolutely not. Why? Because Luke 1:37 says, *"For nothing will be impossible with God."*

I must rethink my position about impossibilities in light of the truth that God can do all things. Jesus made this statement in His first public message, *"Repent, for the kingdom of heaven is at hand"* (Matt. 4:17). What was He saying to them and to us? I think He was saying that in order to accommodate the new order of things that is at hand, they must change their minds about how to know God. He was initiating the new order of things based on His entrance into the world; and because of that, it required everyone to rethink or repent of previously held beliefs. A great adjustment of thinking (that is, repentance) was required.

Repentance certainly includes a rethinking about sin and the consequences incurred because of it, but repentance is never to be limited to the subject of sins. Sin originates in the mind and is given expression through thoughts resulting in actions. If one is really repenting of sin, one must not only repent of the deed but also of the thoughts that produced the deed. If we can change our minds, then the deed will not happen. First Corinthians 2:16 says, *"But we have the mind of Christ."*

We have the ability to think like He thinks, and we will think like He thinks if we continuously repent, change our minds, in light of truth. Romans 12:2 calls this process *"the renewing of your mind."* This glorious process is a gift from God that enables us to produce the fruit of the Spirit and overcome the pull of the flesh toward sin. It also allows us to become free of the practice of sin. Jesus did not die to save us from the penalty of sin only, but to also save us from the power of sin. The truth, and our receiving of it, sets us free! All Christians are called to a life of repentance, and it should be occurring on an ongoing basis. We are to be constantly adjusting our minds in light of new, truthful information.

Actually, it is an enjoyable and very productive process. God is actively engaged in the process of changing our minds that we might think like He thinks. The legalist's view of repentance robs us of the experience of discovering truth taught us by the Holy Spirit who was sent to *"guide you into all the truth"* (John 16:13). According to the legalist's model of repentance, sin is taken care of by feeling badly about it, confessing it to God, asking His forgiveness, and repenting, turning away, from it. True repentance can break the power sin has over us by allowing the Spirit of God to reveal truth to us and renewing our minds in the specific area of deception that is producing sin. He guides or coaches us in becoming like Christ in the way we think. If we become like Christ in the way we think, we become like Christ in the way we act!

For most of my ministry life I worried a great deal about how things were going in our church. Most of us pastors do, I have discovered. This worry and anxiety, even when it was low grade, affected me in various destructive ways. Regardless of how on top of things I attempted to be or how much I desired to trust God and have faith, this incessant worry was frequently present. Pastors have a myriad of things to worry about if we are so inclined. Often I would talk to God about the problems or challenges and be reassured everything would work out, but I was never really free of worry. I saw it as sin and a lack of trust in God. My life was impacted negatively in various ways from being grouchy with Martha or being short with our children, to simply not being the joyous, happy person I was created to be.

One day I was reading in Philippians 4, which I had read many times previously, but had never allowed the truth there to change my mind. But it did that day! I came to verses 6-7 where it says,

> *"Be anxious for nothing, but in everything by prayer and supplication with thanksgiving let your requests be made known to God. And the peace of God, which surpasses all comprehension, will guard your hearts and your minds in Christ Jesus."*

When I read those verses, the Holy Spirit said to me, "You need to repent. You need to rethink, or think again, concerning this worry-filled life of yours!" That day I allowed the truth to enter and transform my thinking in that area of my life. I stopped worrying and began simply asking God to take care of things for me. I don't think the same way any longer. I have nothing to worry about! I refuse to worry about anything.

My life was changed that day, and now I am a carrier of peace rather than worry. I exercised the beautiful gift of repentance the way God designed it to work. True repentance gets at the root of our sin instead of dealing with the behavioral symptoms. Legalism only deals with the surface, behavioral problems; and therefore, there are few lasting victories. If I would have repented for being grouchy, I would never have discovered the real issue that was much deeper.

The next time God asks you to repent, embrace it with joy because a life-changing breakthrough is just around the corner! God never asks us to repent for His sake or for His benefit, but for our sakes and our benefit that we might experience the abundant life Jesus came to give. His intention is to lift us up, not put us down, to empower us with truth, not shame us with guilt. Our heavenly Father is a great and loving Father, and He is not the author of the sham that legalism passes off as repentance.

True biblical repentance is relational in nature. It is an interchange between a loving, caring, and infinitely wise Father and a willing and responsive child who loves, trusts, admires, and deeply respects his Father. Neither of them holds anything back in their conversations and communion with each other, which reveals the depth of their relationship. The Father's motive is to bless the child because He treasures this uniquely and divinely created being who has the exact same DNA as Himself. The Father knows what the child will become as his mind is renewed through revelation of the truth and true repentance takes place. This dynamic process is hardwired into our spirit because we are *"predestined to become conformed to the image of His Son"* (see Rom. 8:29). Accelerated growth begins the moment we, His children, embrace the dynamic process of the renewing of the mind through true repentance.

Remember, repentance is rethinking or allowing one's mind to be changed as truth is revealed through the Word and by God's Spirit. Truth really does set us free! True biblical repentance is the pathway to liberty and freedom, spiritual maturity and peace, and experiencing the thrill of beginning to think like God thinks. The legalist's distorted and limited view of repentance, which focuses on behavior modification and rededication of the flesh, produces bondage, spiritual immaturity, and a lack of intimacy with God. Like an abused child performing for the approval of a distant and stern father, the Christian trapped in legalism trudges on with little hope of escaping the maze of religious rules and the cycle of failure built into the system. As the song lyrics say, "Like a rat in a maze the path before me lies, and the pattern never alters until the rat dies."

An Illustration of True Repentance

The parable Jesus chose to teach the value of each human being God has created, and to show the nature of God's love for each of us, is found in Luke 15:11-32. The parable of the prodigal son also gives insight into how true repentance is designed to work. You probably know the story well, so I won't go into great detail.

The younger of two sons demanded his inheritance from his father and the father divided his wealth and gave the son his share. The son packed up his belongings and traveled to a far country where he soon squandered his estate in loose living. A famine occurred in that country, and the son began to go hungry. He attached himself to a pig farmer, but was soon so hungry he desired to eat the pig food.

Now notice what happened: Luke 15:17 says of the wayward son, *"But when he came to his senses…."* This young man of a loving father sinned against his father, but began the process of true repentance when he came to his senses. He began to think truthfully. Regardless of the source or vehicle truth is delivered through, truth is still truth. Truth can come to us in difficulty! The son had a breakthrough in his thinking; and as mundane as it was in his case, it changed his life. Almost all truth seems mundane after we finally see it.

Anyway, the young son came to his senses and decided it was best for him to go home. Remember, true repentance is for us, to help us, not for God or to help Him. The son prepares his speech to deliver to the father when he gets home. Every indication is that he was sincere in his recognition of his sin even if his motive was to have some food like the hired servants in his father's house. The son begins the journey home with little understanding or expectation of the almost unbelievable grace he will encounter when he gets there.

You do know, don't you, that the *"kindness of God leads you to repentance?"* (Rom. 2:4). The more we understand about the great grace of our God, the more natural and exciting repentance becomes. The most endearing and human element in this story happens next. Now remember, the father in Jesus' parable represents our heavenly Father, and this story is being told by the One who has already spent an eternity with Him and knows Him best.

Honestly, it almost makes me cry just thinking about this gracious and loving father whose son is the most important thing in all the world to him. The father desperately wanted his son to come back home, but he loved him enough to want him back having changed his mind, and he loved him enough not to interfere with the process. God knows that when our misery factor rises above our resistance to truth factor, we will listen to Him!

Now picture this incredible insight into our heavenly Father's heart as revealed by His only begotten Son. Luke 15:20 says, *"But while he was still a long way off, his father saw him, and felt compassion for him, and ran and embraced him and kissed him."* Now imagine the Creator of the universe running toward His child, filled with compassion, aggressively hugging, and kissing over and over again, this formerly wayward but now repentant child. The son got part of his repentance speech out, but the father seemed not to notice because he didn't even acknowledge that the son had spoken to him. Notice the absence of anger and recrimination. There is no mention of what was lost, only rejoicing at the great treasure that was regained.

The father neither demanded nor seemed to want a response that included weeping or sorrow or the deep emotional anguish that legalists require in repentance. One other thing stands out to me. The father did not require the repentant son to perform any sort of penance for his sin. It was never mentioned nor brought up again. It was as if it had never happened.

A trademark of modern legalism practiced in some Evangelical churches is the requirement of penance when repentance is being accomplished. A person must always prove his or her sincerity in repentance by never doing the deed again and by making restitution of some sort. This may happen below the surface and under the radar, but it surely happens. While restitution may need to happen on a human level, it cannot happen between the believer and God. Our sin debt has been paid in full with a currency we do not and never will possess.

The father turned to his servants and told them to, *"Quickly bring out the best robe and put it on him, and put a ring on his hand and sandals on his feet; and bring the fattened calf, kill it, and let us eat and celebrate"* (Luke 15:22-23). The picture of our heavenly Father that Jesus painted for us in this amazing parable is the greatest motivation for true repentance that exists. Who can resist such love and compassion? I'll tell you who—the legalistic elder brother—that's who. He is an offended legalist and mean as a snake! He thinks he has never done anything wrong, but we know better and so does the father. The elder brother refuses to attend the party for his brother because legalists never attend anyone's party but their own. He cannot accept the fact that his father is this kind of man who is so different from himself. He believes his father handled the situation with the younger brother all wrong. He thinks punishment should have been applied instead of greasy grace! Legalists have a hard time with grace! So be it. Let's party anyway!

True repentance is a great gift that has the capacity to transform and renew our minds until we think what God thinks, want what God wants, feel what God feels, and become like Jesus. Welcome to the party of grace hosted by our heavenly Father in honor of those of us who have come to our senses in the pig pen of legalism and decided to come home to be with Him.

Conviction

Does the word *conviction* have a positive or negative connotation to you? I am willing to bet it is negative. Even after years of seeing the truth about conviction, I still fight the condemnation that is associated with a religious understanding of the term. Pastors and teachers in the "sin management" business are deeply dedicated to making sure this "ministry of the Holy Spirit" (as they see it) is embraced by their constituents without question. Since guilt, shame, and the threat of God's punishment are primary weapons in their sin management arsenal, the leaders make sure conviction of sin is seen as the primary function of the Holy Spirit. I am convinced most pastors and leaders do not have evil intentions nor impure motives toward their people; however, they are deceived and have believed the lie of the enemy that behavior modification is the goal God has set before them in ministry.

Because helping people control their flesh through human effort and adherence to rules is not only a thankless but never-ending task, most leaders employ any strategy that promises even a measure of success. Guilt, shame, condemnation, and threats in God's name are presented by the enemy as viable options. The Church has swallowed this lie hook, line, and sinker!

As with confession and repentance, conviction is a concept that is always associated with sin, and because of that close association, the true ministry of the Holy Spirit in the lives of believers is tragically limited. The enemy has his fingerprints all over this lie! He hates the ministry of the Holy Spirit primarily because the Holy Spirit is described by Jesus as the *"Spirit of truth"* (John 16:13). The devil knows the power truth has in unleashing each believer to be conformed to the image of Jesus, and releasing the Church from this web of deceit to become the force that destroys the gates of hell.

The Holy Spirit's role in convicting believers of sin is presented by legalists and modern Pharisees as if there are many biblical references to support this concept. In reality, there are not many biblical references to support the concept that the Holy Spirit's primary ministry is to convict believers of sin. As a matter of fact, there are no New Testament verses that refer to the concept! Furthermore, there is only one verse in the New Testament directly referring to the Holy Spirit convicting of sin and that reference reveals the role of the Holy Spirit in convicting the world of sin. *"And He, when He comes, will convict the world concerning sin and righteousness and judgment"* (John 16:8).

The word translated "convict" comes from the Greek word *elencho,* which means "to convince."[4] The Holy Spirit's ministry to the world is to convince the world of sin *"because they do not believe in me,"* Jesus says in John 16:9. The Holy Spirit has already convinced me of sin, and now I believe in Jesus! He is now convincing me of righteousness (see John 16:10). I am convinced that I am becoming *"the righteousness of God in Him"* (2 Cor. 5:21) The Holy Spirit convinced me of judgment and that truth helped me become a believer. Now He is convincing me that *"the ruler of this world has been judged"* (John 16:11)—not me!

The Holy Spirit came to convict the world of sin, righteousness, and judgment. He is still actively doing what He came to do in reference to the world.

In reference to us, now that we are not of this world but citizens of God's Kingdom, what is He doing? John 16:13 gives us the answer, *"But when He, the Spirit of truth, comes, He will guide you into all the truth."* That does not sound to me like the Holy Spirit's main job is to convict us of sin as the Pharisees among us think. The Holy Spirit is certainly capable and willing to convince us of sin, but that is not the main thrust of His ministry to us. His ministry is to guide us into all the truth, and as we are convinced of the truth, we change our minds (repent) where we have believed a lie or untruth, and the truth sets us free. True convincing (conviction) leads to a change of thinking (repentance), and it happens in an atmosphere of love and acceptance without the presence of condemnation.

The Holy Spirit, Jesus says, *"will glorify Me; for He will take of Mine, and will disclose it to you"* (John 16:14). In other words, the

Holy Spirit will convince the world that the standard of righteousness required to be in union with God is the sinless perfection Jesus demonstrated while on earth. The Holy Spirit convinces believers that we are in a state of being of sinless perfection because of our faith in the finished work of Christ. The Holy Spirit convicts the world of their need of a Savior, and convicts believers that they have a Savior and have become the righteousness of God in Him. See, conviction is a good and positive concept for both groups of people! Conviction of the Holy Spirit is a great positive that goes far beyond and is never limited to the conviction of sin.

What I have observed in my own life and heard from the testimony of many friends is that the limited concept of conviction of the Holy Spirit taught by those who have legalism as a base of belief produces a works-based system of relating to God. True repentance cannot be achieved by a response to condemnation. Condemnation has no place in a believer's thinking. If it is present, you can rest assured it did not come from the Holy Spirit. Condemnation has its source in the kingdom of darkness and is ministered by demons. When a person is born again, that person is translated from the kingdom of darkness into the Kingdom of God's dear Son. There is no condemnation in His Kingdom! (See Romans 8:1.)

I believe that much of the repentance that is done by many believers is, in actuality, a form of penance in response to condemnation rather than true repentance in response to convincing of the Holy Spirit. It is a vicious cycle of "coming clean," but never achieving victory.

How are we really transformed? What dynamic transforms us into the image of Christ? Is it through willpower, looking at the law and being determined to never sin again? Is it through the power of shame and guilt that we are transformed? Legalists would say so. They say if you can make sin look bad enough, believers will quit sinning. I have a Greek word for that philosophy—baloney!

Through what dynamic are we changed? Does the never-ending cycle of remorse for sin, asking for God's forgiveness, committing to never doing it again, and rededicating ourselves to "holy living" ever produce real change? Are we changed by the power of the law, looking at our sin, or by the power of love, looking at Christ and His finished work? You must make a choice! A flesh commitment to law-keeping can modify your behavior for a time, but it cannot transform your life.

Love can transform your life from the inside out. You can spend the rest of your earthly life so breathlessly in awe of God and His love for you that you begin to be transformed into the image of Jesus. In order for that miracle to happen, you must get off the religious treadmill of performance, get out of the maze of legalism, and receive by faith what Christ has accomplished on your behalf. It is not easy to believe because it is so grand and glorious, but it is true. Allow the Holy Spirit to convict you of the truth about the conviction of the Holy Spirit!

I am sure it is apparent by now that these three terms, confession, repentance, and conviction, which represent very important concepts in our spiritual health and growth, are interrelated. All three of them are strategic in allowing the truth to do its work in the transformation and renewing of our minds. Remember, as our minds are renewed, we begin to think like God thinks, and that incredible, miraculous transformation is what the devil most wants to prevent. If he failed to prevent you from being born again, his fall-back strategy is to prevent you from *"grow[ing] up in all aspects into Him"* (Eph. 4:15).

The enemy's primary point of attack to prevent the miracle of transformation through the renewing of the mind is to pervert and, thereby, limit the impact and life-giving power of confession, repentance, and conviction. Those trapped in the lie of legalism have little hope of ever escaping the maze of performance-based Christianity until they get to Heaven. They simply have no chance of becoming the joyous, life-filled, and maturing disciples Jesus died to redeem and the Holy Spirit came to empower unless they change their minds.

LOOK AND SEE

Please, for your own sake, consider the possibility that the Good News is much better than you have previously thought, and that just maybe the devil is behind your present performance-based belief system. If you look, you will begin to see!

This is how God designed the truth to work. The Holy Spirit *convicts* (elencho, to convince) or convinces me that I have believed a lie. I *confess* (homologeo, same word, agree with) or agree with the Spirit of Truth (no sense of condemnation). I then *repent* (metanoia, rethink) or change my mind in light of truth.

This process renews my mind and allows me to think like God thinks concerning any area of life. This process happens in an atmosphere of complete trust between a loving and infinitely wise Father and a willing and trusting child. I trust the motives of my Father to bless me and never condemn me, to accept me and never reject me, to be patient with me and never punish me, to enlighten me and never lie to me—and to always have my best interests in His heart. My love and admiration for Him grows with every encounter, and I become more like Him every time I talk to Him.

I am confident He is changing me through changing the way I think until He is fully reflected through me. The fruit of His Holy Spirit begins to be produced through my transformed life. You can call this process greasy grace if you want to, but realize when you do, you are cooperating with the enemy of Christ and calling into question His finished work.

To all you Pharisees out there, good luck finding your way out of the maze! To the rest of you, welcome to the joyous journey of being *"guided into all the truth"* (John 16:13) by the precious Holy Spirit of God.

ENDNOTES

1. From the song "Patterns" by Simon and Garfunkel.

2. http://www.studylight.org/lex/grk/view.cgi?number =3670; accessed August 3, 2011.

3. http://www.merriam-webster.com/dictionary/metanoia; accessed August 3, 2011.

4. Vines Complete Expository Dictionary – pg. 128

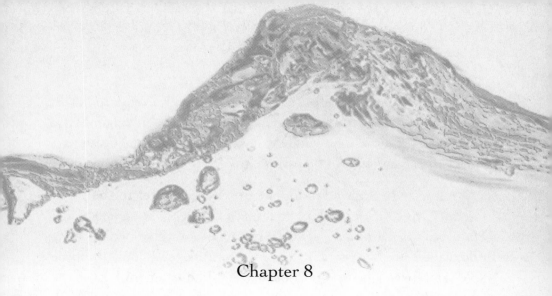

Chapter 8

What About the Law?

But we know that the Law is good,
if one uses it lawfully.
—1 Timothy 1:8

In Chapter 4, we saw that Christians are not under the jurisdiction of the Old Testament Law. Romans 7:6 says, *"But now we have been released from the Law, having died to that by which we were bound, so that we serve in newness of the Spirit and not in oldness of the letter."* It is important for us to understand what our attitude is to be toward the Law.

What place is the Law to have, if any, in our lives as believers? How we view the Old Testament Law and how we apply it is of paramount importance, not only in our personal lives, but in our lives corporately as the Church. There is great danger in relating to and applying the Law in inappropriate ways. One could say it is a matter of life and death. *"… for the letter [Law] kills, but the Spirit gives life"* (2 Cor. 3:6).

What exactly are we talking about when we refer to the Law? John 1:17 says, *"For the Law was given through Moses; grace and truth were realized through Jesus Christ."* The first five books of the Bible, called the Pentateuch, contain what the Jews consider to be the Mosaic Law. The first portion of the Old Testament Law is the Ten Commandments found in Exodus 20, which most people think of when they hear the Law referred to, but there are hundreds of laws governing every aspect of life in the Mosaic Law. The totality of all the laws that make up the Law is what is referred to as the Old Testament Law.

There is a very important truth concerning the Law that Christians must know and never forget. Jesus fulfilled every legitimate requirement of the Law, including the laws governing everyday life—the moral law—and the laws governing the worship of God—the ceremonial law. He also fulfilled all the requirements to observe the feasts of Israel and all other ceremonial observances under the Law. All of them spoke of Jesus prophetically, and in "types" and "shadows" they proclaimed His messianic ministry.

> *Then beginning with Moses and with all the prophets, He explained to them the things concerning Himself in all the Scriptures* (Luke 24:27).

> *…These are my words which I spoke to you while I was still with you, that all things which are written about me in the Law of Moses and the Prophets and the Psalms must be fulfilled* (Luke 24:44).

All of it was about, and pointed toward, Jesus!

We can never see the full revelation and meaning in the Old Testament until we see the Old Testament through the revelation of the New Testament. The Old Testament is the New Testament concealed. The New Testament is the Old Testament revealed. We can now see what the Old is really about because we have the New through which to see it. We can now see that it was all about Jesus! All of this has an important application in how we, as New Testament believers, are to relate to keeping the Law.

Let me give you an example. In our area of the country, there are many believers in a certain denomination who teach and practice "keeping the Sabbath" and believe all Christians should worship on Saturday or the seventh day of the week exclusively. Indeed, the law says to "remember the Sabbath day, to keep it holy" because God accomplished creation in the first six days and rested on the seventh. The commandment was to rest on that day and do no work because God blessed the Sabbath and made it holy.

Are the majority of Christians wrong and in sin by worshiping on Sunday? *No!* Jesus fulfilled the law concerning the Sabbath. What was required of them in the natural, Jesus fulfilled in the spiritual. The New Testament says in Matthew 12:8, *"For the Son of Man is Lord of the Sabbath."* And Mark 2:27 says, *"The Sabbath was made for man, not man for the Sabbath."*

Jesus fulfilled that requirement of the Law and furthermore, there is a spiritual rest that the Old Testament Sabbath spoke of that we are to enter into. *"Therefore, let us fear if, while a promise remains of entering His rest, any one of you may seem to have come short of it.... For the one who has entered His rest has himself also rested from his works, as God did from His"* (Heb. 4:1, 10).

How do we keep the Sabbath spiritually? We rest in Him and make no attempt to work our way into a relationship with God. What they did in the natural under the Law, we do in the spiritual by trusting that Christ's work was sufficient to gain for us what our works could not and cannot gain. Every day is a Sabbath day for us! Every day is a day of worship for us. Every day is a day of rest for us. We should rest all the time! By the way, if you feel you must choose a certain day for corporate worship (you don't, but just in case you do), Sunday, the first day of the week is a good one. It is resurrection day! Christians are not under the jurisdiction of the Law because we are joined to the One who fulfilled the Law and is greater than the Law.

Many Christians are so in bondage to legalism that they not only believe we should observe many Old Testament practices of worship and conduct, but judge others who don't as being in sin. This is all a bunch of religious nonsense that reveals a deep resistance to the revelation of truth. Pharisees are never happy about the liberty and freedom that union with Christ brings to our lives. Read what Paul writes in Galatians 4:9-11:

> But now that you have come to know God, or rather to be known by God, how is it that you turn back again to the weak and worthless elemental things, to which you desire to be enslaved all over again? You observe days and months and seasons and years. I fear for you, that perhaps I have labored over you in vain.

If you want to observe such things and feel the liberty to do so, then go ahead, but don't put those same requirements on anyone else. Paul says in First Corinthians 10:23, *"All things are lawful, but not all things are profitable. All things are lawful, but not all things edify."* Mature believers understand such things and choose to respond in wisdom to the liberty in which we stand just as Christ did and modeled for us.

Since believers are not under the jurisdiction of the Old Testament Law, by what or whom are we governed? Are we in a lawless state of being, free to do without consequences whatever our flesh desires to do? Do we now use our liberty as an occasion for the flesh and see how much we can get away with without paying a price? Many think that is exactly what will happen if grace is embraced as a lifestyle. Some accuse me of teaching such nonsense because they are eager to defend their legalistic view of Christianity in which they have so much invested. They accuse me of being antinomian or anti-law. I view this criticism as a compliment because it puts me in some pretty good company! Jesus must have been accused of being antinomian because He defended Himself by saying, *"Do not think that I came to abolish the Law or the Prophets; I did not come to abolish but to fulfill"* (Matt. 5:17). Apostle Paul must have heard the same antinomian accusation from the Judaizers and responded by writing the Book of Galatians!

Let's go back to the question by what or whom are Christians governed? We are governed by the King of kings and Lord of lords. Under His jurisdiction, the law of love is the law of the land. James calls this law the royal law (see James 2:8). He also calls it the law of liberty in James 1:25. Jesus put it this way:

> *"You shall love the Lord your God with all your heart, and with all your soul, and with all your mind." This is the great and foremost commandment. The second is like it, "you shall love your neighbor as yourself." On these two commandments depend the whole Law and the Prophets* (Matthew 22:37-40).

Christians are governed by Christ, and the Law of His Kingdom is love. I have said it before but it bears repeating; love is the greatest constraining power against sin that exists.

Love is patient, love is kind, and is not jealous; love does not brag and is not arrogant, does not act unbecomingly; it does not seek its own, is not provoked, does not take into account a wrong suffered, does not rejoice in unrighteousness, but rejoices with the truth; bears all things, believes all things, hopes all things, endures all things. Love never fails..." (1 Corinthians 13:4-8).

THE PURPOSE OF THE LAW

How do freedom and grace relate to law and law-keeping? What application does the Law legitimately have in the life of a believer? Again, it is imperative that we understand how we are to properly relate to the Law because a misapplication of the Law in a believer's life is deadly! The Law is like a killer virus that spreads its toxic poison and multiplies itself exponentially until it kills its host.

While the Law has a legitimate role to play in the world and is described by Paul as holy (see Rom. 7:12), it is holy only when it is applied according to its intended purpose. Remember, *"a little leaven* [of the Law] *leavens the whole lump"* (Gal. 5:9).

So what is the purpose of the Law? The following are three purposes worthy of note:

1. The Law brings the knowledge of sin: *"...through the Law comes the knowledge of sin,"* and *"I would not have come to know sin except through the Law"* (Rom. 3:20, 7:7). The Law brings to each of us the knowledge of sin and reveals to us our need of a Savior.

"Therefore the Law has become our tutor to lead us to Christ, so that we may be justified by faith" (Gal. 3:24). The Law plays the necessary role to bring to us the knowledge of sin without which we cannot be justified or saved. Paul calls the Law a tutor or teacher that leads us to Christ. For the contribution to my life that the law has made, I am eternally grateful, for without it I would not know Christ. However, I am now finished with my relationship to the Law. *"But now that faith has come, we are no longer under a tutor"* (Gal. 3:25). The Law is still doing what it has always done; showing the world the knowledge of sin and the need of a Savior.

2. The Law reflects God's opinion concerning moral conduct. How would I know coveting is sin if the Law had not said, "You shall not covet"? What is God's opinion concerning adultery? Is He for it or against it? How would I know if the Law had not said, "You shall not commit adultery"? The Law gives a baseline of understanding about successful living as a human being in the world God created. Allowing the Law to give insight into how God created us to best function as a society is a matter of wisdom. We see at least some reflection of the Law even in the laws that govern us nationally and locally through our civil governments. The U.S. Constitution reflects Judeo-Christian ethics. Even those who do not know Christ are well-served to allow this law to influence and restrain human tendencies toward lawlessness and chaos.

While the Law does reflect God's opinion on matters of moral conduct, it does not reflect the full extent of His love. God's motive behind the giving of the Law was love! He loves us enough to make us aware of our sin and spiritual death and our need of a Savior. God loves us far beyond our ability or willingness to keep the rules. I don't keep rules to earn God's love. He loves me so much that He gave His only begotten Son as a sacrifice for me while I was still a reckless and rebellious lawbreaker. The Law does not reflect the measure or depth of God's love!

An illustration of this magnificent truth is found in John chapter 8. The scribes and Pharisees brought a woman—many believe it was Mary Magdalene—caught in the act of adultery to Jesus to see what He would say in order to accuse Him. They said, *"Now in the Law Moses commanded us to stone such women; what then do you say?"* (John 8:5). Jesus says, *"He who is without sin among you, let him be the first to throw a stone at her"* (John 8:7). They all left one by one until the woman and Jesus were left alone.

In this next exchange between Jesus and the woman, we see the heart of God toward even sinful and law-breaking human beings expressed: *"Jesus said to her, 'Woman, where are they? Did no one condemn you?' She said, 'No one, Lord.' And Jesus said, 'I do not condemn you, either. Go. From now on sin no more"* (John 8:10-11).

There are several points of truth we need to take away from this beautiful and inspiring incident. *One,* Jesus is the only one there that day who had the right to condemn—and He did not! Why? Because He did not come into the world to condemn the world but that the world through Him would be saved (see John 3:17). *Two,* legalistic Christianity has this truth turned backward and therefore robbed of its great power to heal. The legalistic behavior modification gurus say to those who have failed to keep the rules, "go and sin no more and we won't condemn you." Jesus says, "I don't condemn you, go and sin no more." He knew the power of love and its ability to transform a human heart!

Condemnation should have no place in our lives, whether toward others or toward ourselves. Romans 8:34 says, *"Who is the one who condemns? Christ Jesus is He who died, yes, rather who was raised, who is at the right hand of God, who also intercedes for us."*

The rock throwing legalists who fill modern Christian churches and spawn the pharisaical preachers they listen to each Sunday seem to be more dimwitted than the Pharisees of Jesus' day. They, at least, walked away without saying a word and had sense enough to keep their mouths shut, which is more than can be said of the mean-spirited Pharisees of our day.

Jesus' method of confronting sin seemed to work rather well, don't you think? Mary was immortalized in Scripture when she poured out the costly perfume and anointed Jesus' feet and was a devoted, loving, and life-giving disciple to the very end.

Three, God's love extends far beyond His desire for us to be good boys and girls. He loves even if He disapproves! So should we, and so can we! The Law, while reflecting the opinion of God on good behavior, does not reflect the extent of God's love. Can you think of a symbol that does reflect the extent of His love? *The cross!* God's love far outreaches His desire for moral behavior.

3. The Law is a source of wisdom. David says, *"Your commandments make me wiser than my enemies…I have more insight than all my teachers…"* (Ps. 119:98-99). The Law expresses a wise way to live and order one's life and is valuable as a resource for decision making. We must trust that God knows what He is talking about when healthy human behavior is discussed.

WHAT THE LAW IS NOT

Now that we have identified the purpose of the Law, let's explore what the Law is not and does not do.

1. Law-keeping does not justify. John 1:12 says, *"But as many as received Him, to them He gave the right to become children of God, even to those who believe in His name."* Receiving Jesus and His finished work by faith is the only pathway to salvation. Law-keeping does not save.

2. Law-keeping does not sanctify. A commitment to attempt to keep the Law in all of its applications will not produce a life like Jesus'. If law-keeping was the answer to becoming perfect, then the Pharisees would have been good examples of how to live. Jesus says, *"...unless your righteousness surpasses that of the scribes and Pharisees, you will not enter the kingdom of heaven"* (Matt. 5:20). Law-keeping cannot change or transform a person's heart.

3. Law-keeping is not a true reflection of spiritual maturity. It is deception of the highest order to use law-keeping as a measure of a person's spiritual progress or maturity. Again, if law-keeping was a true measure of spirituality, then the Pharisees would be good examples. Jesus says in Matthew 23:27, *"Woe to you, scribes and Pharisees, hypocrites! For you are like whitewashed tombs, which on the outside appear beautiful, but inside they are full of dead men's bones and all uncleanness."* External adherence to the Law does not reveal the true nature and character of a person and should never be used to measure someone's spiritual maturity. Paul writes in Second Corinthians 10:12, *"...when they measure themselves by themselves, and compare themselves with themselves, they are without understanding."*

Legalism always compares performance and is always wrong in its conclusions. Please understand how very deadly legalism and the misapplication of the Law is to the spiritual health and growth of all true Christians. While we all should be appreciative of its work in bringing to us the knowledge of sin and our need of a Savior, once we are saved, the Law must be kept in its proper place and never used inappropriately.

"It was for freedom that Christ set us free; therefore keep standing firm and do not be subject again to a yoke of slavery" (Gal. 5:1). Properly relating to the Law is a matter of life or death!

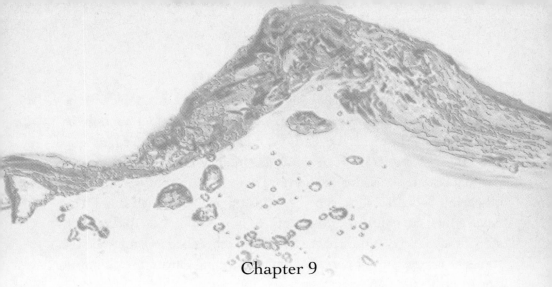

Chapter 9

Saved Completely

He is able also to save [completely] *forever*
those who draw near to God through Him....
—Hebrews 7:25

On the banks of Caddo Lake in Northeast Texas near the Louisiana border, there is a small town called Uncertain. While I have never met anyone from Uncertain, Texas, I can easily imagine the conversations the residents of the town inevitably would have with outsiders, and the one-liner jokes that must be repeated endlessly. It can't be easy living in Uncertain!

One of the most damaging and destructive results of legalistic Christianity is the uncertainty that many true believers live with concerning their salvation. I have actually had hundreds of conversations with believers who are not only uncertain about their salvation, but honestly believe no one can be certain beyond any doubt that they are saved. A "hope so" is the best answer they can give to any inquiry concerning their future destination after death or relationship with God in the present. Many others are only a small step beyond this tragic view of salvation. They believe they are children of God, but could certainly lose that relationship if they fail to "endure to the end." Still others believe and teach that someone can lose his or her salvation by rejecting Christ or by committing some heinous sin such as suicide or murder.

All of this uncertainty produces a weak and ineffective witness to the finished work of Christ and hinders a life of active faith God designed us to live. Such teaching also perpetuates spiritual immaturity and displays a lack of trust in God's ability to keep what is committed to Him. The Body of Christ, in general terms, has a very low view of the divine nature of the new birth resulting in deep spiritual insecurity and profound confusion. In my opinion, the mixture of law and grace which is predominately taught and believed to be true by the Protestant church represents the work of Christ in a manner that is just short of heathenish!

Someone has accurately said that there are only two kinds of religion: the religion of human achievement or the religion of divine accomplishment. You cannot have it both ways! Legalistic Christianity presents God's grace in salvation then turns right around and presents human achievement in the preservation of that grace-given salvation. If someone cannot be good enough to earn salvation, what makes us think someone can be good enough to keep salvation? A mixture of grace and law always, and I mean always, ends up producing religious nonsense that we wouldn't put up with in any other venue in our lives but seem to eagerly go along with in church.

If the devil couldn't keep you from being saved, his fall-back strategy is to keep you in doubt that you are saved. If he failed to keep you from attempting to earn your salvation, he will try to deceive you into attempting to keep it through human effort. If he can no longer control your eternal destiny, he will try to render you ineffective in your ability to influence others toward the glorious reality of union with Christ.

We are going to look at several areas of biblical truth that I believe will help us see that our redemption was complete and thoroughly executed by Christ and that we can add nothing to what He did and is doing. We are helpless to keep what He freely gives, but He will not lose what cost Him His life to secure for us. Since He lives forever, and therefore is our High Priest forever and is forever interceding for us, then we believers are saved forever! Salvation is based on *His* finished work, not ours.

Turning Hope So Into Know So

First John 5:13 says, *"These things I have written to you who believe in the name of the Son of God, so that you may know that you have eternal life."* According to the apostle John, we can know we have eternal life. We should not live our lives in doubt about the eternal life that Jesus died to secure for us. Where many get tripped up is in their observations of others who claimed to know Christ but walked away or returned to a former destructive lifestyle after claiming to be saved. While I am not God and certainly cannot judge whether someone else is a true Christian or an imposter, I do know appearances can fool us. Some are not what they appear to be, and some have even fooled themselves into thinking they are born again when in fact they are not. Jesus says, *"Not everyone who says to Me, 'Lord, Lord' will enter the kingdom of heaven"* (Matt. 7:21).

The reason some walk away from Christ is not because they lost what He secured for them, it is because they never knew Him. John says:

> *They went out from us, but they were not really of us; for if they had been of us, they would have remained with us; but they went out so that it would be shown that they all are not of us* (1 John 2:19).

Now listen to the next verse as John addresses the true Christians. *"But you have an anointing from the Holy One, and you all know"* (1 John 2:20).

Jesus addresses this issue in the parables of the *"sheep and goats"* (Matt. 25:32-33) and the *"wheat and the tares"* (Matt. 13:24-30). The application is simple: True Christians are in a permanent, eternal union with Christ. They have been cleansed of their sin and have become "new creations" in Christ and are already seated with Christ in heavenly places. This dynamic and unalterable miracle was accomplished by the finished work of Christ and His work alone.

Allow me to interject a word of caution. Do not presume to be able to judge the salvation experience of another. While we can suggest that someone might examine whether or not they are born again based on a lifestyle or fruit that does not seem consistent with true Christianity, only God is the ultimate Judge. I have seen true Christians so demonized and confused that they appear to be unsaved, and I have the capacity to appear that way myself at times, but that does not mean the miracle of salvation has not happened. People tend to look on outward appearance, but God looks at the heart. True Christians walking in the flesh can appear to be unregenerate. Non-Christians acting well can appear to be regenerate. My point is that true Christians can rest in the absolute security that Christ provides and allow the truth to renew our minds and become who we already are—like Jesus. Let's look at some life-changing truths concerning our security in Christ.

THE PROMISE OF THE SCRIPTURES

Romans 8:38-39 says, *"For I am convinced that neither death, nor life, nor angels, nor principalities, nor things present, nor things to come, nor powers, nor height, nor depth, nor any other created thing, will be able to separate us from the love of God, which is in Jesus our Lord."* Absolutely nothing can ever separate us from the love of God! To be separated from God's love is the same as being separated from God. Nothing can separate us from God!

John 10:27-30 says, *"My sheep hear My voice, and I know them, and they follow Me; and I give eternal life to them, and they will never perish; and no one will snatch them out of My hand. My Father, who has given them to Me, is greater than all; and no one is able to snatch them out of the Father's hand. I and the Father are one."* Jesus said He knows us. That is a term of union and communion. Our relationship with Him is irrevocable and unbreakable.

Paul uses the term "in Christ" numerous times to show our position as saints. He knows us, and we know Him! Because of that reality, no power in the universe can "snatch" us out of His hand. Being in Christ is as secure as it is possible to be. He has already given us eternal life and we shall never perish! What a glorious truth! To doubt His ability to keep those of us who know Him is to doubt His deity. He claims to be "one with the Father"; and if that is true, He is beyond doubt!

Some have said to me, "But what if I all of a sudden decide I don't want to be a Christian, or that I no longer believe in Jesus, or I just have no desire to have anything to do with God. What happens then?"

My response is that two possibilities are presented. *One,* it is impossible for a true Christian—one in whom the Spirit of God dwells, one who has become a new creation in Christ, one who has been raised from spiritual death to life, one who is the righteousness of God in Christ—to ever reject Christ or ever disbelieve His divinity. Impossible! I have never met one a person like that, and neither have you because they do not exist. Romans 8:16 says, *"The Spirit Himself testifies with our spirit that we are children of God."* That witness to us is so profound and encompassing and compelling that it is irresistible and undeniable. First Corinthians 6:17 says, *"But the one who joins himself to the Lord is one Spirit with Him."* True Christians are one spirit with Christ and could never reject Him. It is simply impossible!

Two, any person who can reject Christ, stop believing, or plunge into a life of rebellion against God without remorse, was simply never born again—regardless of testimony to the contrary. True Christians cannot deny Jesus, and true unbelievers cannot remain with Him.

THE PERFECTION OF THE SACRIFICE

For by one offering He has perfected for all time those who are sanctified (Hebrews 10:14).

Therefore He is able also to save forever those who draw near to God through Him, since He always lives to make intercession for them. For it was fitting for us to have such a high priest, holy, innocent, undefiled, separated from sinners and exalted above the heavens; who does not need daily, like those high priests, to offer up sacrifices, first for His own sins and then for the sins of the people, because this He did once for all when He offered up Himself. For the Law appoints men as high priests who are weak, but the word of the oath, which

came after the Law, appoints a Son, made perfect forever
(Hebrews 7:25-28).

Jesus has perfected for all time those who are sanctified. He was able
to accomplish this magnificent work because He was a perfect Sacrifice.
He also was able to save forever those who draw near to God through
Him. True Christians are saved forever! If someone was capable of being
saved and then "losing" his or her salvation, in order to be saved again,
Jesus would of necessity have to die again. If that were the case, His sacrifice would have to be judged to be imperfect just as the Old Testament
sacrifices were imperfect and had to be repeated each year. If we believe
the lie that a true Christian can become unborn again, then we must also
believe it is impossible for such a person to ever be saved again.

What happens when a true Christian sins? Does he lose his salvation? And if he does lose it, how big a sin does it take to cause this monumental loss? See how nonsensical this all gets when the truth is rejected?
Does a true Christian lose his salvation when he sins? Of course not!
Romans 4:8 says, *"Blessed is the man whose sin the Lord will not take
into account."* And First John 2:1 says, *"And if anyone sins, we have an
Advocate with the Father, Jesus Christ the righteous."* Sin is never "laid to
our account" again. That is such good news it is almost unbelievable! It
is true, though, and is so dynamic that many stumble over it.

I may sin after I am born again, but that sin is not taken into account by my heavenly Father because of Christ's perfect sacrifice.
That is good news to me because I honestly wouldn't trust the best
fifteen minutes I have ever lived to save me or keep me saved!

The Position of the Saints

*Therefore if anyone is in Christ, he is a new creature; the old
things passed away; behold, new things have come* (2 Corinthians 5:17).

Our position as believers is clearly stated as being "in Christ." Paul uses this term or derivatives of it, such as in Him, in the Beloved, or with Him, numerous times to describe where all believers stand positionally. Every human being is abiding or living or positionally situated in one of two spiritual realities. We are "in Adam" or we are "in Christ". If I am "in Adam", everything that pertains to Adam pertains to me. If I am "in Christ" everything that pertains to Christ pertains to me. First Corinthians 15:22 says, *"For as in Adam all die, so also in Christ all will be made alive."*

If I am a believer, I am in Christ and there is no safer place to be! I will die when He dies—and He lives forever. I will be condemned when He is condemned—and that is impossible. I lose my position at the right hand of the Father when He loses His position there. I lose my inheritance when He loses His—and that is never going to happen. I am as secure as He is secure. I repeat, there is no safer or more secure place to be than in Christ!

> *By this, love is perfected with us, so that we may have confidence in the day of judgment; because as He is, so also are we in this world* (1 John 4:17).

As He is, so also am I right now in this world! While I am still waiting for the full expression of Heaven because of my mortal body, I am already a citizen of Heaven and have been seated there from the instant of my new birth. I am not working to achieve it or qualify for it nor working to keep it. I already have it because I am in Christ. I will fall from grace when Jesus does—and that will never happen! My security comes from my position in Christ, not from my position in Heaven.

Many believe and teach a scenario that goes something like this:

I am convicted of sin by the Holy Spirit and trust in Christ as my Savior, and that miracle of salvation happens because of my faith and God's grace. I could not earn salvation by good works; salvation is only possible by grace through faith. Sound good so far? The moment I am saved by grace through faith, I begin a lifetime of attempting to be good enough to earn God's blessings, and a lifetime of hoping I will not stumble so badly that I lose what I gained in trusting Christ as my Savior. When I sin, I must immediately confess it, repent of it (commit to never doing it again with God's help), and pay whatever restitution that is required; because if I die with that sin unconfessed and unrepented of, I might not make it to Heaven. There is always the possibility that I could deny or reject Christ as my Savior and thereby nullify my salvation; therefore, I must hang on to Christ with everything I have. If I make it through life without blowing it too badly and serve Christ enough to gain some favor with God, when I stand before Him in judgment, He will say "Welcome to My Heaven." Then the gates to Heaven slam shut behind me. I then can finally exhale a big breath and relax and feel secure. I might have earned only a small cabin in Heaven, but at least I'm there. My coattails were smoking, but I made it!

Whether this scenario is actually believed by its proponents or not, the people in the pews are seeing it that way, and they are seeing it that way because that is exactly what they are hearing. Whether the denomination is Evangelical or Pentecostal, some version of this religious, lying garbage is being taught and believed by its hearers. As my dad used to say, "It is a steaming pile of horse manure, so don't step in it." What an unmitigated mess we have made of the glorious Gospel of Christ. Our security doesn't come from getting out of earth and into Heaven. The angels fell from Heaven! Our security doesn't come from a place, it comes from a Person. Our security comes from being in Christ! We are in union with Him and are sons and daughters of God! We are not waiting or hoping that will happen, it has already happened, and nothing can change it. We are as secure here and now in Christ as we will be then and there in Christ!

Many believe we must work to keep our salvation. Those same people believe we could not work to get our salvation. If good works could not procure our salvation, why would good works secure our salvation? Listen, our security is not based on the quality of our commitment to Him; our security is based on the quality of His commitment to us! Legalism always ends up being nonsensical and grace always makes logical sense when seen clearly. I have often thought that if you believe that someone can lose the salvation secured by grace through faith, when someone prays to receive Christ the best thing to do would be to pull out a gun and blow him away on the spot. Then He would be in Heaven with no chance of "losing" it! It would be better to be in Heaven than run the risk of losing salvation by continuing to live. As I said, legalism is nonsense.

AN ILLUSTRATION OF SECURITY

Remember, we are discussing the position of the saints as being in Christ and have concluded that there is no safer or more secure place to be than in Him. A great illustration of this amazing truth is found in Genesis chapters 6 through 8 in the account of Noah building an ark. One interesting detail in this story is in Genesis 6:8, *"But Noah found favor* [grace] *in the eyes of the Lord ."* This is the first time the term "grace" is found in the Bible and gives us a perfect illustration of salvation by God's grace.

The ark is a type or representation of Christ. Peter confirms this in First Peter 3:20. The flood was God's judgment against sin, and the ark was a vessel of safety and security for those who found grace in the eyes of God. Genesis 6:14 says, *"...you shall...cover it inside and out with pitch."* Pitch is a tar-like substance that Noah used to seal the cracks of the ark so the water, judgment, could not enter; and he placed it on the inside and outside of the ark. The Hebrew word translated "pitch" is the word *kapar*. Kapar is translated over 70 times in the Bible as the word atonement. We know from a New Testament perspective that Christ's blood atones, or cleanses, us of sin. It keeps us safe from the judgment of God against sin. The pitch Noah applied to the ark symbolizes the blood of Christ and its atoning work on our behalf.

I believe this story is beyond doubt all about God's judgment against sin and the security that Christ provides through the atoning work of His shed blood on the cross. Now, notice another truth in this amazing story. Genesis 7:16 says, *"Those that entered, male and female of all flesh, entered as God had commanded him; and the Lord closed it behind him."* This is a reference to the single door that Noah had built in the ark according to God's plan. When the animals and then Noah and his family entered the ark, God closed the door. Noah didn't close the door—God closed it! They were sealed in the ark!

Ephesians 1:13-14 says:

> *In Him, you also, after listening to the message of truth, the gospel of your salvation—having also believed, you were sealed in Him with the Holy Spirit of promise, who is given as a pledge of our inheritance, with a view to the redemption of God's own possession, to the praise of His glory.*

True believers are sealed with the Holy Spirit "in Him." The Holy Spirit was also given as a pledge or earnest payment of our inheritance. God has promised us an inheritance and given us the Holy Spirit as a pledge on that promise!

Let me tell the story of Noah and the ark from perspective of our friends who believe we can lose the redemption that Christ died to provide. God said to Noah, "I am about to destroy every living thing on the earth with a flood. You have found grace in My eyes and therefore I will save you and your family. Build an ark and put some pegs on the outside for yourself and Mrs. Noah and your family to hang onto during the flood. Hang on with all your might. Pray for strength to hold on faithfully to the end and you will be saved."

I have actually heard people ask for prayer to be able to hang on until the end! What an impossible task, and an utterly demoralizing view of the finished work of Christ many present as truth. Listen, Noah may have fallen down inside the ark many times, but he never fell out of the ark because he couldn't get out if he had wanted to, which he didn't because he wasn't insane! My ability to preserve my salvation is just as impossible as my ability to secure it in the first place. He secures it for me because I am sealed by the Holy Spirit "in Him." Jesus is my Ark of safety.

The Present Tense of Salvation

When a person is born again, the Bible describes the results of that new birth as the person having passed out of death into life. That new life is, by definition everlasting, eternal. Eternal life is the only kind of spiritual life in existence. There is no such thing as temporary eternal life!

Jesus says in John 5:24:

Truly, truly I say to you, he who hears My word, and believes Him who sent Me, has eternal life, and does not come into judgment, but has passed out of death into life.

Jesus is not describing an event that has its culmination in Heaven or at some point in the future when we have grown beyond temptation or have somehow passed some unknown test. He clearly states that believers have eternal (King James Version says "everlasting") life at the moment of the new birth experience. Any time spiritual life is referred to in the New Testament, the reference is to eternal life because there is no other kind of spiritual life. Eternal life, once entered into, is a permanent state of being.

Jesus says to Martha in John 11:25-26, *"I am the resurrection and the life; he who believes in Me will live even if he dies, and everyone who lives and believes in Me will never die. Do you believe this?"* Did you notice the statement, "and everyone who lives and believes in Me shall never die"? True believers will never die because we live in Him and believe in Him! To lose your salvation is to die—and that cannot happen. Once eternal life is entered into through the experience of the miracle of the new birth, by definition it can never end or it was not eternal to begin with.

For example, did Adam and Eve have eternal life in the Garden of Eden before the Fall? No. How do I know? Because they sinned and died as a result! If the life they had was eternal, it would never have ended. Suppose I was saved for ten years then did something that caused me to lose my salvation. During that ten years did I have eternal life? No, I had only ten years of life, and therefore it wasn't eternal at all. All spiritual life is eternal because God is eternal and He is the Giver of life. One cannot come into and go out of eternal life.

Either one has eternal life or no life at all. Every true Christian has eternal life now, and that will not and cannot change. The difference in Adam and Eve and New Covenant believers is the life Adam and Eve had was secured by their obedience. The life we have is secured by Christ's obedience.

THE PRAYERS OF THE SAVIOR

There are layers upon layers of security our heavenly Father has put in place for each true Christian. One source of security that many never consider or never interpret correctly is the fact that Jesus, as our High Priest, is continually praying for us. While we have covered the truth of Jesus' high priestly ministry in a previous chapter, a focus on the results of that ministry is needed.

Hebrews 7:24-25 states the fact of Jesus' priesthood and then at the end of verse 25 this awesome statement is made, *"since He always lives to make intercession for them."* We have a *"minister in the sanctuary, and in the true tabernacle, which the Lord pitched, not man"* (Heb. 8:2). Jesus has *"taken His seat at the right hand of the throne of the Majesty in the heavens"* (Heb. 8:1) and He is interceding for us. He is not only praying for us, but interceding for us with His shed blood and resurrected life!

An insight into the content of at least some of Jesus' prayers for us comes from His "High Priestly prayer" in John 17. In verse 9 of John 17 Jesus prays, *"I ask on their behalf; I do not ask on behalf of the world, but of those whom You have given Me; for they are Yours."* Then in verse 11 He prays, *"...keep them in Your name, the name which You have given Me, that they may be one, even as We are."* We begin to see the protective nature of Jesus toward all of us who know Him. And listen to John 17:15 where Jesus prays, *"I do not ask You to take them out of the world, but to keep them from the evil one."* Jesus prayed, and is still praying, that we be kept from the evil one who He knows hates us and would destroy us if he could.

You do know, don't you, that the evil one would seduce you away from Christ if he could? Some believe the devil can "snatch" us out of Christ's hands through his powers of seduction and treachery. Please know this about the enemy of our lives, if he could "reclaim" us, he would. If he could, he would! If he could and simply hasn't, it is because he hasn't chosen to, and if that is the case you are going to Heaven by the grace of the devil. No! The only reason he has not stolen us back from Jesus is because he cannot. We are "kept from the evil one" and he cannot touch or tamper with the eternal life we have in Christ. Jesus is our High Priest, and He is interceding for each of us 24/7/365. He is not only praying for us, but interceding for us on the basis of His perfect, sinless life, His sacrificial death, and His victorious resurrection where He took back the keys of death, hell, and the grave from the enemy of our lives. Our eternal lives are secure because of that glorious, finished work by the King of kings and Lord of lords! I will "fall" only when He "falls"—and that, my friend, will never happen.

Never allow the devil to deceive you into thinking your salvation or the securing of it is based on the quality of your commitment to Christ. Your salvation and the security you have in Him are based on the quality of His commitment to you, and He is committed to you with everything He has. *"I am the good Shepherd; the good Shepherd lays down His life for the sheep"* (John 10:11).

THE POWER OF SOVEREIGNTY

All would agree that God's power is limitless and that He rules and reigns over every aspect of His created universe. None of us is so prideful and ignorant to ever believe we have full understanding of

God's omnipotence because such power is beyond our comprehension. The little we do know of it leaves us breathless and speechless with wonder. He created everything that exists out of nothing with a spoken word. God is powerful!

When God's power is applied in any measure to any purpose, all that God desires to happen is accomplished. Agreed? With that in mind, read First Peter 1:3-5:

> *Blessed be the God and Father of our Lord Jesus Christ, who according to His great mercy has caused us to be born again to a living hope through the resurrection of Jesus Christ from the dead, to obtain an inheritance which is imperishable and undefiled and will not fade away, reserved in heaven for you, who are* **protected by the power of God** *through faith for a salvation ready to be revealed in the last time.*

Did you notice the phrase "protected by the power of God"? The King James Version translates the phrase "kept by the power of God." Another viable translation would be "guarded by the power of God."

We are kept, protected, or guarded by the power of God until such time as our glorious inheritance is fully released into our possession. This inheritance is imperishable, beyond defilement, will never fade away, and is reserved in Heaven for us. Those of us who have been born again to a living hope through the resurrection of Jesus Christ from the dead, through faith in Him and His finished work, are protected by the power of our omnipotent God until we inherit there what has already been secured for us here! Deal with that, devil!

Some of us have the silly and somewhat prideful thought that we have the power to undo what God's power is guarding and preserving. Our heavenly Father will never allow us to be able to forfeit what cost His Son His life to secure. The covenant that covers and guards our eternal life is based on Jesus' perfect and sinless life—not on our feeble and powerless attempts to keep ourselves from falling away. We are protected by the power of God and we are utterly, absolutely, and completely secure.

Your inheritance is waiting for you and it is your Father's joy to give it because it cost His only begotten Son's life to secure it for you. You are *saved completely!*

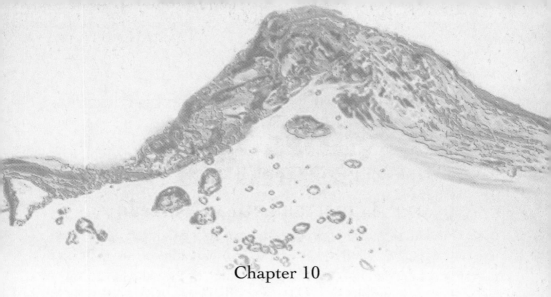

Chapter 10

The Next Great Awakening

Awakening—an act or moment of becoming aware;
to rouse from sleep.

I believe the Body of Christ is on the threshold of a new spiritual reformation that will impact the world in much greater measure than the Protestant Reformation. The Protestant Reformation, beginning in the 16th century, led by Martin Luther, John Calvin, Ulrich Zwingli, and others, reestablished the truth of the Gospel concerning salvation by grace through faith. That spiritual awakening almost single-handedly propelled the Church and the world out of the dark ages and established a spiritual framework the Protestant church has operated under for the past 500 years.

Perhaps the monumental impact the Protestant Reformation had is the primary reason few ever saw the fundamental flaws in its theology. As I stated in the introduction to this book, little has changed in the core belief system, methods of evangelism and discipleship, or in the fundamental way God is perceived by the Church in the past five centuries. The Church has adapted to changing culture in its appearance somewhat, but the core presentation of the truth concerning one's salvation and ongoing relationship with God is the same as it was in the 16th century: One is saved by grace through faith and then begins a life of human effort to modify behavior to meet standards imposed by whatever religious authority one is submitted to in order to please God or to avoid causing damage to God's reputation. Some spiritual authorities are more liberal and easygoing than others, but never doubt that there are standards of behavior—and meeting those standards is the whole point of the religious exercise. Ultimately, it comes down to behavior as a gauge of spiritual maturity and one's ability to please God. Much more grace is extended to unbelievers than to those who have been saved by God's grace and have become God's children.

After more than 40 years of being part of the Protestant church, I am convinced this is an accurate representation of things as they are in the understanding of most Christians today. I have some good news for those who have suffered quietly and tried their best to go along with this legalistic mess we have made of the glorious Gospel of Christ. Things as they are in the Church are about to change!

The Spirit of Truth is actively engaging the minds of many in our day as He did with Martin Luther and others in the 16th century. A reformation of centuries of incorrect thinking and a reformation of a belief system rooted in legalism is underway and will not be silenced or sidetracked. It is growing in influence and will exponentially multiply until the second coming of Christ. The revelation that will produce this great reformation in the Church is the revelation of grace, the revelation of the finished work of Christ, and the revelation of God as our Father.

A pristine example of the Church operating in this revelation is the Church described in Acts chapters 2 and 4. The early Church is characterized by great joy, liberty, and awe of the grace of God. Their fellowship, focused around their common union with Christ, was rich and awe-inspiring. They were *"continually filled with joy and with the Holy Spirit"* (Acts 13:52) and *"abundant grace was upon them all"* (Acts 4:33). *"And all the more believers in the Lord, multitudes of men and women, were constantly added to their number"* (Acts 5:14).

There is a longing in the heart of every true believer to live in the liberty and be filled with the joy that Jesus died to provide. There is also an inner knowing that something about the legalistic Christianity experienced by most believers is seriously flawed in its foundation. The gap between the early Christians and what most of us have experienced is simply too great to ignore. Something is wrong and needs to be corrected!

An understanding of God's great grace will correct what is wrong and will produce the results Jesus promised when He says, *"I came that they may have life, and have it abundantly"* (John 10:10). There is a disconnect in the theology of Protestants that produces a low grade but consistent dissatisfaction among most believers regardless of what commitment level they have to God. If you listen closely to the conversations among believers as they discuss spiritual issues in their lives, you will recognize the signs of discontent and dissatisfaction.

Even the most dedicated and devoted disciples express frustration with their ability to fully connect with God on an ongoing basis and need frequent doses of inspiration to remain engaged in spiritual disciplines such as Bible reading or prayer, not to mention the weightier spiritual issues such as the exercise of spiritual gifts or hearing God's voice. The only real answer to this dilemma that they hear is to "try harder," "be more disciplined," or "get more involved in the church." While I am not against discipline or church involvement, the problem is a faulty theology, not faulty commitment. The leaven of the law embraced by Protestants has left the Body of Christ vulnerable to confusion and robbed us of the wonder and awe of life with God.

Satisfaction in life flows primarily out of an understanding of who we are, not what we do. The Gospel was designed and executed to produce in us satisfaction, a sense of fullness, and a deep inner connection with God that leaves little room or desire for expressions of our flesh. John Piper said, "Sin is what you do when your heart is not satisfied with God."[1] How can I be satisfied with a God who is always disappointed with me?

Jesus says in Matthew 5:6, *"Blessed are those who hunger and thirst for righteousness, for they shall be satisfied."* Blessed means happy or blissful. Happiness or blessedness is a result of Christ's righteousness satisfying us at the deepest level of our being. Being blessed means we will be fully satisfied. Our hunger and thirst for right standing with God is fully satisfied in Christ, and we are happy as a result. Understanding our identity in Christ and our union with God transforms us into the image of Christ. Christian legalism robs us of that happiness and satisfaction because under its tyranny there is always more to do to earn favor with God. We find ourselves in a perpetual state of discontent rather than experiencing the absolute fullness and satisfaction Christ's righteousness provides.

The more I learn of the finished work of Christ, the more I see that He is satisfied with me because I believe! I am a favored son of God, and His presence satisfies me beyond anything else in life.

Haven't you ever wondered why the most joyful, excited, and spiritually alive believers among us are the new ones? I was that way back then and probably so were you! Honestly, I am grateful I didn't grow up in the church. How sad is that? See, I remember how I felt as a new Christian. I remember the freshness, the newness, and the unhindered joy I felt in being accepted by this great God I had come to know. I also remember the lifelong struggle to return to that beautiful, uncomplicated, joyous, life-filled relationship with my heavenly Father that came naturally to that little babe in Christ.

A deadly flaw in the theology of Protestantism, which teaches that I am saved by grace through faith but perfected through the flesh (human effort), robbed me of a lifetime of unimpeded spiritual growth. Many times I have wished that I could start over knowing what I know now! Since that is impossible, I am determined to be part of the oncoming wave of truth-tellers and life-givers who are waking up to the revelation of God's great grace.

There is a coming Great Awakening to the Body of Christ that will be resisted fiercely by the legalistic establishment which has so much invested in the sin management model of discipleship, but it will be embraced with joy and great enthusiasm by the mass of deeply dissatisfied, spiritually tormented, and tired of playing the game believers who make up the majority of the Protestant church. Notice what Paul says in Second Corinthians 4:15:

For all things are for your sakes, so that the grace which is spreading to more and more people may cause the giving of thanks to abound to the glory of God.

The Spirit of Truth is loose among us, and He is revealing what has been hidden under centuries of religious lies. Grace is indeed "spreading to more and more people" and causing "the giving of thanks to abound to the glory of God."

BIBLICAL BASIS FOR THE NEXT GREAT AWAKENING

The Feasts of Israel

The feasts that God commanded Israel to observe each year give us prophetic insight into what is ahead for the Church. Before we look at some of the specific details, allow me to jump ahead and state one conclusion I have concerning the fulfillment of the last feast, which is the Feast of Tabernacles.

In the last days, there will be greater revelation concerning God being our Father. There will also be a spiritual experience available to every Christian who is willing to receive the fullness of God as our Father. The Feast of Tabernacles is the last feast chronologically and the only one that hasn't yet been fulfilled spiritually in the Church. But just as surely as the others have been fulfilled, the last one will be too! I believe we are in the beginning stages of that great spiritual awakening right now! Let us back up a little and look briefly at the feasts and their spiritual fulfillment in our lives.

God commanded Israel to gather three times during each year to celebrate and commemorate great miraculous events in their history with God. The feasts are described primarily in three portions of Scripture: Deuteronomy 16, Exodus 23:14-17, and Leviticus 23.

In the first month of the year they were to celebrate the *Feast of Passover.* Passover is a "three in one" feast, made up of Passover,

Unleavened Bread, and First Fruits, and lasted for seven days. Exactly 50 days after Passover, in the third month of their religious calendar, they were to keep the *Feast of Pentecost*. In the seventh month, the last month according to their religious calendar, they were to keep the *Feast of Tabernacles* or Booths. Tabernacles is also a "three in one" feast, made up of Trumpets, Day of Atonement, and Tabernacles.

These feasts all have historical, prophetic, and spiritual significance. They give historical context and prophetic insight into the plans of God concerning His Church and His people. Please understand I am summarizing a huge amount of information, and encourage you to study the amazing details of the feasts on your own.

We are interpreting the feasts and applying the truths in them in three ways. We will look at the historical fulfillment of them in Israel, the prophetic fulfillment of them in Jesus, and the spiritual or experiential fulfillment of them in the Church and in our personal lives as believers. They were not just history lessons or archaic religious rituals, they are revelatory events that speak of Christ, salvation, the New Covenant, the Holy Spirit, and ultimately the revelation of God as the great, loving, kind, and good Father that I am coming to know Him to be.

Before we look at the individual feasts and the prophetic meaning of each, I want to state the premise of this chapter. The Feast of Passover reveals the person and work of Christ, the Son of God— God the Son. The Feast of Pentecost reveals the person and work of the Holy Spirit—God the Spirit. The Feast of Tabernacles reveals the person and work of God—the Father. The first two feasts have been spiritually fulfilled. The last one has not, but it will be, and I believe we are in the beginning of that great revelatory work of God now. Greater revelation of God the Father is coming to the Church and to all Christians who will look and see. It is magnificent and life-changing. It is so powerfully personal, so gloriously real, and so thoroughly captivating that it will not only change us, but through us will change the world.

Millions of people will come into the Kingdom. Tabernacles is a season of great harvest to the extent that the reaper overtakes the sower. This revelation of God as Father can only be seen through the lens of unadulterated grace. A law-free understanding of the Gospel is necessary to see and then embrace our heavenly Father as He reveals Himself to be in the New Covenant. If the leaven of the law is present in a person's understanding of the Gospel, a distorted and limited view of God the Father is the result. The grace revealed and promised in the New Covenant is corrupted when the law is mixed in with it. What many call balance is, in truth, a mixture. Protestantism has for centuries taught a mixture of law and grace, and that mixture has corrupted the true Gospel resulting in a Church that is spiritually fatherless.

Dudley Hall, a long-time friend, once stated that he believed the Church to be "over mothered" and "under fathered." I believe he is correct. My take-away from thousands of conversations with believers over the past 40 years is that they see God the Father much different from how they see Jesus and the Holy Spirit. They perceive Jesus as their sacrificial Savior and have a sense of closeness with Him because of His incarnation, His perfect life, and sacrificial death for them. This ability to embrace Jesus and feel close to Him comes from a correct understanding of the Gospel concerning salvation. The Protestants got it right in their understanding of justification by grace through faith. The resulting ability of Christians to fully embrace Jesus as their Savior and Lord comes from the truth of grace without mixture of law. In most Christian's minds and hearts, Jesus is correctly seen as our heavenly Brother. I have no problem with that representation of Him, even though He is so much more.

I have a more difficult time characterizing Protestant believers' understanding of their relationship with the Holy Spirit because they are all over the map! The extremes might be easier to see, with most somewhere in the middle. One extreme is to functionally ignore the Holy Spirit because of the fear of being seen as a nutcase! The other extreme is to be so biblically unsound in their understanding of the person and work of the Holy Spirit that they *are* functional nutcases! I have met plenty from both extremes. The leaven of the law always produces confusion and distortion of the Truth in any area of spiritual life, as evidenced by the extremes of thought about the person and ministry of the Holy Spirit. Seeing the Holy Spirit through the lens of grace without mixture of law allows revelation of the Holy Spirit and His work to become clear—but that is the subject for another book.

I believe the majority of Protestant believers view the Holy Spirit in somewhat of a motherly role. The Holy Spirit provides comfort, nurture, and reassurance of well-being. He is always there to extend kindness, understanding, and healing. He teaches us, warns us, and empowers us to do better. He is sensitive and easily offended, but caring and kind. Sound about right? In other words, He fulfills the role that most relate to their earthly mothers.

Again, I have few problems with that characterization of the Holy Spirit as far as it goes, but there is so much more. As I am sure you realize by now, we have the structure of a family in our minds as we try to fit the Trinitarian nature of God into an understandable and relatable human context. There is me, and I am a son or daughter, brother or sister, then there is an older brother, and a mother. This is a natural and biblical concept because those terms, outside the mother reference, are terms used in Scripture to describe spiritual relationships.

Now let's look at the view most who have lived their lives under the mixture of law and grace have of their heavenly Father. Some will have difficulty admitting we have these thoughts about God, but I am convinced they are an accurate representation of our view of Him. While most Christians agree that God is our spiritual Father, they do not think He is a very good one. Many think He is demanding, stern, distant, unyielding, uncaring at times, and more interested in our good behavior than anything else. If the truth were told, many of us believe He is unfair in His judgments and often rewards people who are not as deserving as others. He punishes us when we sin and withholds His presence and fellowship as a means of correcting us. He is always serious, and having fun is beneath Him. His sense of humor is strongly controlled at best and absolutely lacking at worst. He is big, and fearsome, and scary, and unknowable. He demands deference and humility if we show the temerity to come into His presence. Many see "the fear of God" as the one human quality that impresses Him most. Frankly speaking, He seems to be unappeasable and almost abusive in His relationship with His children. He always demands of us a little more than we are presently giving or doing, and we see no end to it until we get to Heaven.

The leaven of the law has corrupted the truth about our heavenly Father. Something is amiss in our understanding of our heavenly Father if He is seen as a worse father than I am! Many of the qualities in this horrible list are actually taught in one way or another from the pulpits of many Protestant churches. I am certain that much of what we have believed about God as our Father is believed because those we trusted to tell us the truth about Him have taught us that this is what He is like.

We need a new reformation of thought and a great awakening to the truth about our heavenly Father. This great awakening is on the way and it will change our understanding of God in ways beyond our expectations. Grace without mixture of law is the starting place for the next great awakening.

The Feasts of Israel prophetically speak to this revelation of Father God. Let's look at each of them briefly. *Passover* commemorates the historical event of the death angel "passing over" each Jewish household as the exodus out of Egypt was about to begin (see Exod. 12:1-14). Passover prophetically speaks of Jesus. The blood of the lamb applied to their houses was a sign, and no plague would destroy any in the household. Jesus is our Passover Lamb, and His blood applied cleanses us of our sin, and we pass from death to eternal life. Passover speaks prophetically of the miracle of salvation. Every time someone is saved, Passover is kept spiritually.

Unleavened Bread commemorates the eating of unleavened bread during the night of the Passover event. Unleavened bread prophetically speaks of the unleavened or perfect life of Christ. Spiritually for the Church, unleavened bread speaks of the Gospel being taken or eaten without the leaven of the law. After someone is saved (Passover), the person is to eat the unleavened Word without mixture of the law (see Gal. 5:9). As someone eats of the true Gospel, that person is capable of growing up into the *"measure of the stature which belongs to the fullness of Christ"* (Eph. 4:13). We must put out the leavening of the law!

First Fruits commemorates the passing of Israel through the Red Sea after they left Egypt. This miracle speaks prophetically of Christ's death, burial, and resurrection and then His ascension into Heaven. God not only took Israel out of slavery, He took them out to take them into the Promised Land. God not only takes us out of death, He takes us out to take us into union with Him! Jesus became the First Fruit of all the spiritually resurrected ones to follow. Jesus was a Forerunner for all of us! Spiritually, the Feast of First Fruits is kept each time a believer is water baptized, which is symbolized by Israel's passing through the Red Sea.

The *Feast of Passover,* including Unleavened Bread and First Fruits, speaks of the finished work of Christ in justification. We are saved by His perfect (unleavened) life, His vicarious death (shedding of blood), and His victorious resurrection. Salvation can only be received by faith without any human works. This glorious and liberating truth was restored to the Church in the Protestant Reformation. There is no leavening of the law in Protestants' understanding of how one is saved, and the fruit of that pure truth is evident. Testimonies abound, including my own, testifying to the finished work of Christ in salvation. There is great joy, gratitude, and awe at the love of God pouring forth through the Church concerning the miracle of salvation. The reason this fruit is so precious and good is because it is based on truth and grace without mixture of law.

However, the Church has a very different testimony concerning sanctification, or how one is perfected into the likeness of Christ. This is where drudgery, guilt, shame, and human effort enter the picture. The leavening of the law corrupts the pure Gospel at the point of sanctification and produces a life-robbing element into the finished work of Christ. We are back to human effort in an attempt to do what only Christ could do and, in fact, what He has already done. Passover reveals the person and ministry of Jesus—God's Son. That revelation has been restored to the Church. Every week in almost all Protestant churches, there is an invitation given to receive the finished work of Christ by faith unto salvation. This is so because it is the truth without mixture, and we see it, and we believe it. That fundamental truth will never again be stolen, hidden, or taken away. The truth without mixture about sanctification is being restored and will result in a new reformation as surely as the restored truth about justification produced the Protestant Reformation.

The *Feast of Pentecost* was to be kept by Israel exactly seven weeks plus one day after the end of First Fruits (see Deut. 16:12). The event in their history that they were to remember was the experience they had with God at Mount Sinai. Exactly 50 days after passing through the Red Sea, they came to the base of Mount Sinai. There they received the Ten Commandments, rebelled against God, built the golden calf, and suffered judgment as a result. There was wind and thunder, lightning and fire. It is interesting that exactly 3,000 men died at Mount Sinai because of judgment, and 3,000 were born again on the Day of Pentecost in Acts 2. In Second Corinthians 3:7, Paul calls the law *"the ministry of death in letters engraved on stones."* There was death at the giving of the law at Mount Sinai, but life was the result when the Holy Spirit came on the Day of Pentecost. Second Corinthians 3:6 says, *"...for the letter kills, but the Spirit gives life."*

The Feast of Pentecost was prophetically fulfilled in Jesus. He sent the Holy Spirit to us exactly 10 days after His ascension into Heaven. The disciples were commanded to go to the city of Jerusalem and wait for the coming of the Spirit, and they waited for 10 days. After Jesus' resurrection but before His ascension into Heaven, He appeared on earth for 40 days.

Exactly 50 days passed from the time of Jesus' resurrection until the coming of the Holy Spirit on the Day of Pentecost. The Israelites were in Jerusalem to keep the Feast of Pentecost 50 days after Passover. It is interesting that the disciples waiting in the upper room received the reality of which the ritual speaks! The Jews were going through the ceremony of Pentecost, but the disciples were receiving the Person of Pentecost, the Holy Spirit. At the Feast of Pentecost, the Jews were to remember the giving of the law. On the Day of Pentecost in Acts 2 we see the end of the law and the beginning of the

New Covenant. Spiritual Pentecost says we are no longer slaves but sons and daughters! The revelation of Pentecost has been restored to the Church. The person and ministry of the Holy Spirit are seen, at least in some measure, by many Protestants.

In the feasts, God has given us a remarkable road map to follow and the ability to chart a course toward the fullness of all Jesus died to give. He also gives us some insight into future revelation and events. He shows us how to be born again, how we are to grow up by eating the unleavened Word (no mixture of law), and the need for and meaning of water baptism in the Feasts of Passover, Unleavened Bread, and First Fruits.

We are not to stop there, however, because there are more feasts to keep! Every born-again believer should also keep the Feast of Pentecost by being filled with the Holy Spirit. Supernatural anointing and the release of spiritual gifts and manifestations are available to be received, and they are needed in the ministry God has for each of us. When the person and ministry of the Holy Spirit is seen through the lens of grace without mixture of law, the Church will embrace the Holy Spirit with enthusiasm and be able to accurately see the fruit of His ministry through us. Instead of being a point of controversy and confusion, the ministry of the Holy Spirit will unify and empower the Church.

There is a progressive nature to the feasts that will culminate at Tabernacles. Most interpret *Tabernacles* as an end-time feast because it is celebrated in the last month of the religious calendar. We are moving toward Tabernacles and the glorious visitation of God of which it speaks, but we are not there because it has not been fulfilled.

Look at the progression of fruitfulness and ever-increasing revelation of God the Father in the feasts in these examples of tabernacles.

The Tabernacle of Moses is made up of:

- Outer court—Brazen altar of sacrifice and brazen laver speaks of Jesus and salvation. 30-fold Christians. (Passover)

- Inner court—Golden lampstand with oil speaks of the Holy Spirit. Altar of incense speaks of spiritual worship. The Table of Shewbread speaks of the Holy Spirit; illumined Word. 60-fold Christians. (Pentecost)

- Holy of Holies speaks of God the Father and intimacy with Him. Corresponds to the Feast of Tabernacles, a feast of glory, restoration, unity, gladness, and great harvest! 100-fold Christians!

There is a progressively increasing measure in the release of God's work and fruitfulness through His Church and people as we come to the "last days" period of time. It is seen in the groupings of these found in Scripture. Here are a few examples where this "increase" is seen:

Passover—planting—showers of rain

Pentecost—early rain—small spring harvest

Tabernacles—latter rain—abundant year end harvest (Joel 2)

Little children—young men—fathers (1 John)

Mount Goshen—Mount Sinai—Mount Zion (Hebrews 12)

Foolish virgins—wise virgins—Bride of Christ

Blade of corn—ear of corn—stalk of corn

Fruit—more fruit—much fruit

Servants—priests—kings

It is obvious that in Tabernacles we get the greatest expression of the life of God! What I desire to express and show primarily is that there is a revelation of God and a resulting intimacy with Him that will reveal Him as the great Father that He is. This revelation by itself will awaken the Church and allow the Church to experience the joy and liberty that is our birthright.

We are all headed somewhere with Him, and He has the way mapped out for us. We must get to know Him and experience His absolute and pure grace to be able to receive what He desires to give. I don't pretend to know very much, but what little I have discovered about Him and His grace has completely and thoroughly captured my heart, changed the way I read and interpret Scripture, revolutionized my concept of prayer, released the joy of God in my life, inspired me to trust Him in practical ways, and allowed me to receive His undiluted and unrestrained love.

My magnificent heavenly Father loves me without reservation and delights in every discovery I make concerning Him. I am part of a holy and divine family and nothing could possibly be better that that!

This life is available for you as well—but it will only come as you remove the leaven of the law out of your thinking concerning your relationship with God.

ENDNOTE

1. John Piper, *Future Grace* (Multnomah, NY: Multnomah, 1998).

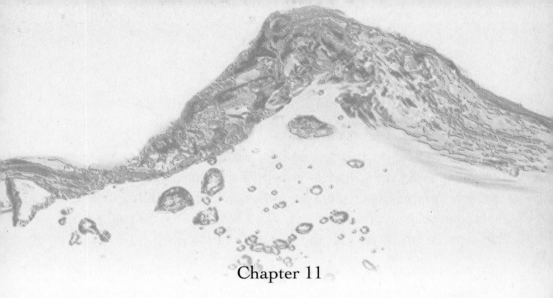

Chapter 11

Father God

There is no disagreement among true Christians, regardless of denominational affiliation, that Scripture presents God as being our heavenly Father. Literally hundreds of New Testament verses present God and our relationship with Him in this manner. Jesus on numerous occasions addresses God as His Father and reveals God to be our Father as well. There is no doubt or disagreement about this truth. Where disagreement comes into the picture is over what kind of Father God is presented to be.

Legalism mars the portrait of our heavenly Father that the New Covenant has painted of Him. A revelation of grace is a necessity for this marred and grotesque misrepresentation of Father God to be corrected, and the beautiful and life-giving truth of our heavenly Father to be restored to the Church.

Apostle Paul, in two separate letters, refers to God in the most endearing and personal terms. I believe these terms reveal the New Covenant's representation of God as Father. Perhaps Paul was echoing how Jesus addressed the Father in the Garden of Gethsemane when He used the terms "Abba Father." Paul says in Romans 8:15:

*For you have not received a spirit of slavery leading to fear again, but you have received a spirit of adoption as sons by which we cry out, "**Abba! Father!**"*

Then in Galatians 4:6:

*Because you are sons, God has sent forth the **Spirit of His Son** into our hearts, crying, "**Abba! Father!**"*

The "Spirit of His Son" cries out through us in this way! In two different languages, *Abba* from the Aramaic and *Pater* from the Greek, we cry out *"Abba ho Pater"* which being translated means, "Father dear Father!" Through the "spirit of adoption as sons" and "the Spirit of His Son," we cry out "Father dear Father." The New Covenant reveals God to be a dear, dear, Father. God is our heavenly Father and He desires a relationship with us that is not only familial but personal and intimate. Religious legalism presents God in a much different light that is not biblical or true.

In the next pages, I present our Father God in a few ways that will give you at least a beginning understanding of what He is really like as a Father. I pray our spirit of adoption as His sons and daughters may begin to cry out "Abba Father" to our great God and Father—because to know Him is to love Him!

GOD IS LOVE

First John 4:8 says, *"The one who does not love does not know God, for God is love."* It is not only that God loves, but He is love! That fact about God is manifested in His sending His only begotten Son into the world so that we might live through Him (see 1 John 4:9).

> *See how great a love the Father has bestowed upon us, that we would be called children of God; and such we are...* (1 John 3:1).

Love has its source in God. All of God's attributes, such as omnipotence, omniscience, and omnipresence, are a foundation for Him to express who He is—and He is love! He has the power to love in ways beyond our human ability to conceive because He is all-powerful. He can creatively and knowledgably love because He knows everything. The measure of His love is limitless because He is infinite. His love will never end or change because He is eternal and immutable. The revelation that God is love has the power to obliterate every legalistic stronghold and any lingering sense of alienation from God that any believer has lived with or suffered through because of religion.

God loved us by faith. He loved us before we loved Him. *"But God demonstrates His own love toward us, in that while we were yet sinners, Christ died for us"* (Rom. 5:8). He "believed" that such a demonstration of His love for us would be responded to and reciprocated! It is the very nature of God to love.

God's love is unconditional. He loves us before we perform! He loves us even if we don't perform. Performance is to better our own lives, not to better His love for us. Our love for Him is a response to His love for us, not the other way around. We can love because He is love and *"because the love of God has been poured out within our hearts through the Holy Spirit who was given to us"* (Rom. 5:5). Love is unconditional. Feelings may be conditional; affection may be conditional; trust may be conditional. God's love is *unconditional!* He loves the world even if the world rejects Him.

Nothing can separate us from God's love. Let me repeat that, nothing can separate us from God's love! In Romans, Paul says:

> *For I am convinced that neither death, nor life, nor angels, nor principalities, nor things present, nor things to come, nor powers, nor height, nor depth, nor any other created thing, will be able to separate us from the love of God, which is in Christ Jesus our Lord* (Romans 8:38-39).

You may think what you did separated you from God's love, but it did not. You may think what you thought separated you from God's love, but it did not. Some preacher may lead you to believe that God is withholding His love, but He is not. May I tell you, God's love and your willingness to receive it, is your singular hope of becoming like Him. Not only have you not been separated from God's love regardless of what you have done or will do, but the revelation of that unmerited and ceaseless love is your lifeline to victory over your flesh. Never allow anyone to cut you off from God's love! The only thing that can limit the love of God is your inability or unwillingness to receive it.

The fact that God is love explains many things and answers several questions concerning our heavenly Father.

1. It explains why a self-existent and self-sufficient God created human beings. God did not create us because He needed us. God created us because He desired to express His love. God did not *need* us, He *wanted* us!

2. It explains free will. Unless love is a free response, it is not love. God doesn't demand we love Him, but He created

us to respond willingly to His demonstrated love for us. We don't have to love Him, but if we get to know Him, we will love Him!

3. It explains redemption. If God was only law and justice, He would have left us dead in our sin. Because He is love, He responded to our spiritual death and helplessness with the greatest act of love imaginable.

4. It explains the existence of Heaven. Because of His great love, everything He is and everything He has He desires to share with us. Love is the motive behind everything our heavenly Father does—without exception! Heaven isn't just a place. Heaven is Him!

I am convinced, as was the apostle Paul, that absolutely nothing can separate us from God's love. He will not allow it!

> *The grace of the Lord Jesus Christ, and the love of God, and the fellowship of the Holy Spirit, be with you all* (2 Corinthians 13:14).

GOD IS GRACIOUS

Father God proclaimed Himself to be gracious in Exodus 34:6, *"The Lord , the Lord God, compassionate and gracious, slow to anger, and abounding in lovingkindness and truth."* God is the Source of all grace, and He is full of grace (see John 1:14). In the New Covenant, God has freely bestowed His grace upon us in the Beloved (see Eph. 1:6). God, being rich in grace, has now lavished His grace upon us in Christ (see Eph. 1:7-8).

God, being eternal, is eternally gracious. Before the world was created, God was gracious. His grace was present before there was anyone to receive it! The creation was planned with grace in mind. *"He chose us in Him before the foundation of the world, that we would be holy and blameless before Him"* (Eph. 1:4).

God's grace fills the universe and is so abundant it rises above the level of anything that attempts to diminish it. Even sin cannot diminish God's great grace! *"…where sin increased, grace abounded all the more"* (Rom. 5:20). God's grace reigns supreme in the New Covenant!

Our heavenly Father has a plan to unveil the extent and abundance of His grace in the ages to come. It will take an eternity to reveal the riches of His grace! When God says He is rich in something, it is unimaginable how much of that substance exists.

> *But God, being rich in mercy, because of His great love with which He loved us, even when we were dead in our transgressions, made us alive together with Christ* **(by grace you have been saved),** *and raised us up with Him, and seated us with Him in the heavenly places in Christ Jesus, so that in the ages to come He might show the* **surpassing riches of His grace in kindness toward us in Christ Jesus** (Ephesians 2:4-7).

I don't know about you, but that truth gives me goose bumps every time I read it! As big and powerful and eternal and smart as my heavenly Father is—all of His attributes, focused on showing us the riches of His grace throughout the ages to come—that leaves me speechless! Our heavenly Father is love, and He is rich in grace. Hot dog!

GOD IS HOLY

God's holiness is mentioned in Scripture more than any other of His attributes. Someone counted roughly 637 references to God being holy. We see a scene in Heaven where God's holiness is recognized in Revelation 4:8:

> *And the four living creatures, each one of them having six wings, are full of eyes around and within; and day and night they do not cease to say, "Holy, Holy, Holy, is the Lord God, the Almighty, who was and who is and who is to come."*

The seraphim in Isaiah's vision also had six wings and declared a similar truth, *"Holy, Holy, Holy, is the Lord of hosts, the whole earth is full of His glory"* (Isa. 6:3). Those in Heaven are impressed with God's holiness!

The New Testament word translated "holy" is from the Greek *hagios*. It means to be "set apart," "completely separate," "pure and morally blameless."[1] The basic idea is difference—that which is holy is different or uncommon. God being holy means He is not only without the presence of evil or impurity, but He is full of what is pure and good and right. Here is the good news for us concerning the truth that God is holy—we never have to worry about God doing the wrong thing!

Here is an abbreviated list of some things of God that Scripture declares are holy: His name, His power, His temple, His Spirit, His covenant, His promises, His city, His ground, His actions, His words, His angels, His prophets, and His people. Yes, His people are holy!

> *But you are a chosen race, a royal priesthood, a holy nation, a people for God's own possession, so that you may proclaim the excellencies of Him who has called you out of darkness into His marvelous light* (1 Pet. 2:9).

We have been made holy as He is holy. One cannot stand in God's presence otherwise. That's just the way God is! He is utterly and absolutely holy, and He had to cleanse us of our sin in order to come into union with us. He cannot accommodate sin in His presence. The leaven of the law has robbed us of a proper understanding of our heavenly Father and His attribute of holiness. Most believers are somewhat put off by the thought of God being holy because they don't see the finished work of Christ in making them holy. God's holiness is intimidating unless one understands that we have been made to be like Him. That is what being righteous means. I am in right standing with God through Christ's imputed righteousness to me.

You are like Him, my friend, and are in a permanent and unchangeable state of being of holiness. It cannot be any other way. God's holiness is one of His most attractive and irresistible attributes. If you will study the scenes of Heaven in Revelation, you will begin to get a picture of the absolute awe that God's holiness engenders in those present. God is awesomely and gloriously holy! He can do no wrong, think no wrong, and every intention of His heart and every action He takes are pure and right and good. He is an awesome Father, and He welcomes you into His holy presence. You are a child of the holy God!

GOD IS SOVEREIGN

I am the Lord , and there is no other; besides Me there is no God. ...That men may know from the rising to the setting of the sun that there is no one besides Me. **I am the Lord , and there is no other** (Isaiah 45:5-6).

Every time God says He is the only God, He is declaring His sovereignty. Sovereign means supreme. He is supreme and fully independent of all others. Besides Him, there is no other. He possesses the highest authority and answers to no one. God only answers to Himself. He is the Supreme Authority in the universe having *"formed the* earth and made it" (Isa. 45:18). God does what is right and best and asks no one what they think about it. He is subject to no one, influenced by none, and is absolutely and completely independent. God does only as He pleases and always as He pleases.

No one or no thing can hinder Him, compel Him, or stop Him. Only one thing seems to move Him—the prayers of the saints. Our heavenly Father is sovereign! Our God reigns!

God has supreme authority to fulfill His plan, and He is absolutely in control of this universe and everything in it. He is completely and totally in charge! Our heavenly Father's sovereignty brings peace and confidence to our lives. I am so very glad He is in charge. I trust Him because of His attributes. I am at peace because He is sovereign. When the Word says, *"God causes all things to work together for good to those who love God, to those who are called according to His purpose"* (Rom. 8:28), I believe He can and will do exactly what He says.

God's sovereignty gives us confidence He has the right to fulfill His promises without consulting any other. Contrary to what we sometimes think, there are no loose ends with God's plans for us or for His universe. Everything is progressing as He has designed and nothing can thwart His intended purposes. I can be at peace because my Father is in charge!

Can you imagine an earthly king giving up his throne and becoming a pauper in order for everyone in his kingdom to become kings? Our great King did exactly that! One phrase in Scripture declares His sovereignty better than any other: "King of kings"! (See Rev. 17:14, 19:16.)

> *Do not be afraid, little flock, for you Father has chosen gladly to give you the Kingdom* (Luke 12:32).

GOD IS GOOD

"You [God] *are good and do good"* (Ps. 119:68), David saw the truth about our Father God. Believe the truth he spoke, and it will change your life! There would be a monumental shift in the Church's belief system if the Church would embrace the truth that God is good and only does good. Everything God has to give, or has given, everything God has done or ever will do, is good because God is good. James says it well:

> *Every good thing given and every perfect gift is from above, coming down from the Father of lights, with whom there is no variation or shifting shadow* (James 1:17).

Our heavenly Father is good, and He does good!

Many years ago I read the newspaper cartoon Dennis the Menace and this particular one was filled with great spiritual truth. The cartoon shows Dennis and his friend Joey walking up the sidewalk to Mr. and Mrs. Wilson's house. When they arrived and knocked, Mrs. Wilson greets them and invites them inside. The next frame shows the boys seated at a counter and Mrs. Wilson is serving them milk and cookies. The boys are then shown leaving and walking down the sidewalk away from the house with Joey asking Dennis, "What did we do good to get cookies?" Dennis' answer is one I have never forgotten, "We didn't get cookies because we are good. We got cookies because Mrs. Wilson is good."

We don't get the good and precious gifts of our Father because *we* are good; we get them because *He* is good!

God is completely good. Everything God is—He is completely! In Exodus 33:18-19, Moses asks God if He will show Himself to him, *"Then Moses said, 'I pray You, show me Your glory!' And He said, 'I*

Myself will make all My goodness pass before you.'" The glory of a person is the essence of who that person is. The summation of a person is his or her glory. When Moses asked God to show him His glory, what God showed him is astounding. Out of all the things God could have shown Moses, He chose to show him "all of His goodness"! God, show me who you really are, Moses requested. God's answer, in essence, was that He is good.

Everything God is, He is completely. All of His attributes flow from His goodness. God is infinite, and that means He is infinitely good. God is immutable or unchanging. He is, therefore, unchangingly good. God is omnipresent, or present everywhere. Therefore, His goodness is everywhere. God is omniscient or all-knowing. Therefore, He is intelligently and purposefully good. God is omnipotent or all-powerful; therefore, He is powerfully good and has the ability to fill the universe with His goodness.

The root word translated "good" is the Anglo-Saxon word—god![2] The Anglo-Saxon word for God is "The Good." When one says, goodbye one is really saying, "God be with you"! God and good go together!

All of creation was an expression or an extension of God's goodness. Genesis 1:31 says, *"God saw all that He had made, and behold it was very good."* Creation was not simply well made, it was good because the Creator is good!

When the leaven of the law is present in our understanding of the Gospel and, therefore, human merit enters the picture, God's goodness is often questioned. I challenge you to trust in God's goodness regardless of what circumstantial evidence might testify to the contrary. We must believe and trust that God is good; and if He could change negative circumstances within the confines of His sovereignty and wisdom, He would. We know He will one day *"wipe away every tear"* (Rev. 7:17) and restore every lost or stolen blessing forfeited in the fallen world in which we live. Until that time comes, trusting in His goodness glorifies Him and goes a long way toward healing us of every hurt we have. God's goodness will rectify every wrong in time. Jesus says:

> *These things I have spoken to you, so that in Me you may have peace. In the world you have tribulation, but take courage; I have overcome the world* (John 16:33).

Our heavenly Father is good and forever will be good. He is a good Father!

The Wow Factor

Several years ago I had the opportunity to have breakfast with a cosmologist (the science of the origin of the universe) who was a guest lecturer at our local university. This guy is a brilliant man and a passionate Christian, and we quickly struck up a friendship. As we began our conversation, I felt rather intimidated talking about a subject I only knew enough about to be dangerous! My new friend was kind and accomodating as we discussed the Old Earth and New Earth theories of creation. All of a sudden he interjected into the conversation a question I thought was a little off subject.

"You do know the universe is expanding, don't you," he asked.

I stammered out an answer that, "Yes, I have heard it is expanding at the speed of light."

He said, "Yes, at the speed of light in all directions!" I had not thought of that. He continued, "The universe is expanding at the rate of 186,000 miles per second in all directions, and has been from the moment God spoke it into being."

I said, "Wow" or some such wise-sounding response.

My friend asked, "Do you know why it is expanding?"

"Uh…no, I certainly do not," I replied.

His voice became strident, his eyes began to gleam, and he said rather loudly, "Because it isn't big enough!"

"It isn't big enough?" I asked.

He repeated the statement, "No, it isn't big enough."

I just gulped and sat there trying to look intelligent. What he said next impacted my life from that time onward. My friend said, actually nearly shouted, "The universe is expanding at the speed of light in all directions because it isn't yet big enough to contain all the things God has prepared for those who love Him!"

"Holy Cow!" I said.

Then we both, with tears in our eyes, began to pray and thank our heavenly Father for His goodness.

God, my friend, is *good!*

ENDNOTES

1. http://strongsnumbers.com/greek/40.htm; acessed August 4, 2011.

2. www.bibleanswerstand.org/God.htm

About Clark Whitten

Pastor Clark Whitten has pastored three mega-churches in his 35 years of pastoral ministry: Gateway Church in Roswell, New Mexico; Metrochurch in Edmond, Oklahoma; and Calvary Assembly in Winter Park, Florida. In 2005 Pastor Whitten planted Grace Church in Longwood, Florida and it has grown to 500 members. For many years Pastor Whitten has traveled America encouraging churches through revivals, conferences, and speaking engagements. He serves on the Board of Directors of Marriage Today and Exodus International. Pastor Whitten's life message is the revelation of grace.

Contact Grace Church at
www.graceorlando.com